D0132693

09-CBF-007

JUMP INTO JAZZ

JUMP INTO JAZZ

THIRD EDITION

A PRIMER FOR THE BEGINNING JAZZ DANCE STUDENT

MINDA GOODMAN KRAINES
Mission College

ESTHER PRYOR
Solano Community College

MAYFIELD PUBLISHING COMPANY

Mountain View, California

London • Toronto

Library of Congress Cataloging-in-Publication Data

Kraines, Minda Goodman.
    Jump into jazz: a primer for the beginning jazz dance student /
Minda Goodman Kraines, Esther Pryor — 3rd ed.
        p. cm.
    Includes bibliographical references and index.
    ISBN 1-55934-549-7
    1. Jazz dance.   I. Pryor, Esther.   II. Title.
GV1784.K73 1996   96 — 19679
793.3 — dc20   CIP

Manufactured in the United States of America
10 9 8 7 6 5 4 3 2

Sponsoring editor, Serina Beauparlant; production editor, Melissa Kreischer; manuscript editor, Melissa Andrews; art director, Jeanne M. Schreiber; art manager, Robin Mouat; text designer, Donna Davis; illustrator, Kristin Mount; cover designer, Ellen Pettengell; manufacturing manager, Amy Folden. This text was set in 10/12 Galliard by ColorType and printed on 50# acid-free Ecolocote by Malloy Lithographing, Inc.

Cover photo: Courtesy Cathy Roe, © Cathy Roe Productions. Image modified by Ellen Pettengell.

 This book was printed on acid-free recycled paper.

CONTENTS

Chapter Seven

BASIC JAZZ DANCE   97

Chapter Eight

MOVEMENTS TO CHALLENGE THE BEGINNING DANCER   127

Chapter Nine

PUTTING IT ALL TOGETHER   139

Chapter Ten

FITNESS FOR THE JAZZ DANCER   155

Chapter Eleven

THE DANCER'S INSTRUMENT: TAKING CARE OF IT   165

PREFACE

Since the publication of the second edition of this book in 1990, jazz dance continues to be an integral part of the entertainment field. It remains highly visible on television specials, music videos, and commercials. Jazz dance enriches live performances on the Broadway stage and in regional and local theater, and it is the captivating force behind touring dance and theater groups. Elaborate jazz dance productions are a vital aspect of many music concerts, and at the cinema, jazz dance continues to enliven movie musicals. In the 1990s, jazz dance has expanded its venue to include the entertainment and cabaret shows found at vacation resorts, on cruise ship lines, and in theme parks.

In addition to constituting an enthusiastic jazz dance audience, jazz dance continues to capture the attention of adults, teenagers, and children as a form of recreation and as a way to fitness.

Whatever the dancer's motive, jazz dance is appealing because of its energy and variety. Jazz dance movements can be sharp or smooth, quick or slow, exaggerated or subtle. Jazz dance can be expansive leaps or contained turns. Its movements can reflect and inspire a variety of moods. Jazz dance is energy in motion, vital and vibrant.

Jump into Jazz attempts to meet the needs of the novice dancer by summarizing a substantial body of basic dance techniques and principles, with easy-to-follow examples and illustrations. We hope it will serve as a guide for the beginning student as well as a reference for all those interested in jazz dance.

Jump into Jazz begins with an in-depth narration of jazz dance's lively history and the most up-to-date information on jazz dance in the 1990s. Chapter 2, "Getting Started," then describes appropriate dance attire, class etiquette, and the structure of a typical class. Our introduction to jazz dance continues in Chapter 3 with a discussion of the dancer's alignment. The discussion defines correct alignment and addresses postural deviations that may affect the dancer. This is followed by a series of appropriate alignment exercises with particular emphasis on the correct care and alignment of the back.

In this new edition, Chapter 4 presents the basic ballet movements and principles that are used in the jazz dance class, and Chapter 5 describes basic jazz dance positions. We have expanded Chapter 6 to include proper stretching techniques, as well as a series of standing and floor stretches. A new feature is an in-depth discussion of strength-building exercises for the abdominals and upper torso. To help the student put these basics together and dance, Chapter 7 discusses steps, turns, aerial movements, and floorwork. New to this text is information in Chapter 8, which is dedicated to movements that will challenge the beginning dancer. Chapter 9 presents basic music theory as it applies to dance and focuses on the importance of space, dynamics, projection in dance performance, and jazz dance choreography.

Because dance is as much a demanding physical activity as it is an art form, fitness as it applies to the jazz dancer is the topic of Chapter 10. An expanded discussion of fitness includes new information regarding training principles, body composition, and techniques for weight assessment.

Chapter 11 continues the topic of fitness with injury prevention, first aid for dance injuries, and nutrition. New to this chapter is information regarding eating disorders that unfortunately can plague dancers. Remedies are outlined for success in weight control. Additionally, exercise as a means for stress reduction is a new topic in health care for the dancer.

Chapter 12, "The Dancer's Next Step," provides dancers with insight to additional training and tips for a successful performance as well as the business and backstage elements of the performance scene. For the aspiring dance professional, we have expanded the topic of a future in jazz dance. The appendix provides an overview of jazz dance styles.

For their helpful suggestions and advice we wish to thank: Kym Atwood, University of West Florida; Joy Burkhart, Baylor University; Cynthia P. Ensign, University of Northern Iowa; Sue Gilson, Palomar College; Mary Jo Horvath, Southwestern University; Mary Maitland Kimball, Indiana University-Purdue University at Indianapolis; Jaye Knutson, Towson State University; Dana Lichty, University of Northern Iowa; Nina Maria Lucas, Illinois State University; and Mary Deweese Mory, Longwood College. We would also like to thank Maria P. Cleary, Kelly Garcia, and Elizabeth Redican for their time and effort as models for our illustrations. Finally, a special thank you to James Claffey for his advice and his photography contributions.

This third edition is dedicated to Guy, Denaya, and Marissa Kraines for their love and support and to John Silva for his continued love and support.

Our hope is that, after reading this book, you will surely want to jump into jazz!

Clockwise from left: Luigi, Matt Mattox, Joe Tremaine, Frank Hatchett,
Gus Giordano.

CHAPTER 1

JAZZ DANCE: A HISTORY

American choreographer Agnes de Mille described the vital spirit of jazz dance as "the true American pep, creativity, and fun." The bond between jazz dance and the United States is more than spiritual, however: Jazz dance mirrors the social history of the American people, reflecting ethnic influences, historical events, and cultural changes. Jazz dance has been greatly influenced by social dance and popular music—especially jazz music. The two jazz forms evolved together, each echoing and affecting developments in the other.

The varieties of jazz dance reflect the diversity of American culture. But, like so much that is "from America," the history of jazz dance begins somewhere else.

THE BEGINNING

The origins of jazz music and jazz dance are found in the rhythms and movements brought to America by African slaves. In Africa, every event of any consequence was celebrated and expressed in music and dance. The style of African dance is earthy: low, knees bent, pulsating body movements emphasized by body isolations and hand clapping. As arriving slaves, Africans from many cultures were cut off from more than their artistic conventions; they were isolated from their families, their languages, and their tribal traditions. The result was an intermingling of African cultures that created a new culture with both African and American elements.

Laws supported by southern slave owners prohibited slaves from playing African drums or performing African dances. However, the prohibition of their native music and dance did not suppress the slaves' desire to cling to those parts of their cultural identity. The rhythms and movements of African dance endured in foot stamping and tapping, hand clapping, and rhythmic voice sounds.

1

MINSTREL SHOWS

In the nineteenth century, American whites discovered that they enjoyed the music and dance that the slaves had created. In minstrel shows, white entertainers parodied their conception of slaves' lives and popularized the African style of dance and music, which depended greatly on solo performance and improvisation.

After the enactment of the Fugitive Slave Act of 1859, many blacks migrated north, where they replaced black-faced white minstrel performers. For the most part, though, the minstrel show was a southern entertainment—until it incorporated the cakewalk. Originally, the cakewalk was a social dance invented by blacks. Couples paraded in a circle, creating intricate steps in competition for the prize of a cake—hence the name *cakewalk*. Minstrel shows began to incorporate a theatrical form of the cakewalk as the grand finale, and many of the shows were a success nationwide. The$sense of competition was retained by couples marching elegantly around in a circle, showing off with high kicks and fancy, inventive struts.

With the popularity of minstrel shows and the development of vaudeville, white performers, still in imitation of black dancers, introduced the buck-and-wing. This dance was strongly influenced by the Irish jig and the English clog, with their fast legwork and footwork and minimal body and arm movement. The buck-and-wing was unusual: The dancer's movements stressed the musical offbeat, or upbeat. This metrical pattern was typical of African music, which is often counted one-**two** rather than the traditional European way, **one**-two. The popularity of the buck-and-wing encouraged musicians to create new accompaniments that employed the unusual rhythm, which is known as *syncopation*. The syncopated music that resulted came to be known as jazz, and syncopation was—and still is—its hallmark. As the music evolved, so did the dance. Dancers adapted the movements of the buck-and-wing and incorporated them to create the elegant and graceful soft-shoe.

With white dancers as the star performers of the minstrel and vaudeville shows, it was difficult for a black dancer to gain stature as part of a troupe. Embittered, many black performers migrated to Europe, where they introduced the newly evolving forms of jazz music and jazz dance. In Europe, these talented and innovative performers were received more readily than in their American homeland. The minstrel show eventually evolved and was absorbed into the twentieth-century musical comedy.

At the close of the minstrel period, the syncopated rhythms of American ragtime bands accompanied the introduction of early forms of jazz dances. In the brief period from 1910 through 1915, over a hundred new dances emerged and disappeared from American ballrooms. The most significant of these dances were the fast-paced, hectic, one-step dances. The public outrage caused by these wild dances paved the way for the fa-

The Joffrey Ballet's interpretation of the cakewalk. Photo by Martha Swope.

mous dance team of Vernon and Irene Castle. The Castles brought an elegance to the dances of the period with the refined Castle walk and made dancing a fad in high-society circles. They also popularized a new dance step, the fox-trot. Inspired by the rhythmic style of the blues, the fox-trot outlasted all the other dances of the period. When World War I started, the public was engaged in the novelty of dancing in restaurants and cabarets, which gave a great impetus to the musical craze called jazz.

THE 1920S

The 1920s marked the end of World War I, and Americans looked forward to a period of prosperity. The dances that emerged during this period reflected the public's need for gaiety and freedom, which were lacking during the war era. Through the end of the 1920s, Dixieland jazz music, with its fast ragtime beat, spread from New Orleans to Chicago

The wild Charleston set the world dancing in the 1920s. Photo from New York Public Library at Lincoln Center.

Bill "Bojangles" Robinson, light on his feet and full of charisma. Photo from New York Public Library at Lincoln Center.

and New York. The growth of jazz dance was directly influenced by this musical genre.

For a brief time, exclusively black casts danced to jazz music on the Broadway stage in such musicals as *Shuffle Along* (1921) and *Runnin' Wild* (1923). *Shuffle Along* introduced the dynamic dancer and performer Josephine Baker. Baker was in the chorus line but immediately called attention to herself with mugging and out-of-step movements that were done with such finesse that they became a featured part of the act. She continued to dance on Broadway until she went to Paris, where she became a huge success. Many other black performers also found success in Paris at this time.

Runnin' Wild introduced the Charleston, and Americans were quick to adopt it. In the Charleston, dancers used body isolations for the first time in a social dance, and the hand clapping and foot stamping that it incorporated were a direct link to the dance's African origin. The Charleston popularized dancing and prompted new dances such as the Big Apple and the Black Bottom, which were performed to dance songs that included dance-step instructions in the lyrics.

This was also the era of Bill "Bojangles" Robinson, a black tap dancer who achieved world fame through the clean and clear percussive rhythms of his feet. The early versions of tap dance evolved from the Irish jig, which incorporated limited upper body movements. As the movements of tap dance became more flexible, the lightness of Robinson's style influenced the future of tap dance by changing the placement of the tap steps from the full foot to the ball of the foot. Bojangles was seen performing on Broadway, in Hollywood films, and in shows that toured the country. His recognition helped to establish the popularity of this dance form.

THE 1930S

The 1920s closed with the introduction of talkies, and the public flocked to the movie houses and abandoned the Broadway musical. The 1930s were the years of the Depression, when people sought an escape from their dreary lives. They found escape in dance marathons and big bands. Dance competitions became popular, for people were willing to try anything in the hope of winning a cash prize. Jazz music moved away from ragtime, Dixieland, and blues, and a new sound began to emerge with the "symphonic jazz" of Paul Whiteman. He brought full orchestration to his music and made syncopation a part of every song he played. The substitution of countermelodies for improvisation made his music more danceable.

The black American bands of Duke Ellington and Louis Armstrong also attracted public attention. Their music gave birth to swing, and a line from a song by Duke Ellington tells how quickly Americans took to it: "It don't mean a thing if it ain't got that swing." The swing era, also termed the big-band era, was marked by the orchestrated jazz music of such greats as Artie Shaw, Glenn Miller, Benny Goodman, Tommy and Jimmy Dorsey, and Count Basie. Swing music consisted of a simple theme that was improvised on by solo instruments. The dances that evolved during the swing era were an interpretation of the energy that this musical style generates. During this time, the Savoy Ballroom in Harlem, dubbed "The Home of Happy Feet," was the largest ballroom in the world—one square block—and for thirty years jazz dancers and swing musicians converged there.

Well-known dances that emerged from this era were the jitterbug and the boogie-woogie. The boogie-woogie was characterized by knee swaying and foot swinging. The jitterbug, initially introduced as the Lindy-Hop (named in honor of aviator Charles Lindbergh), was a syncopated two-step or box step. After the basic step of the Lindy, the couples separated for the breakaway, the improvisational section of the dance. During the middle and late 1930s, these improvisations became a show unto themselves. The steps and improvisations of the Lindy brought back the solo style of dancing characteristic of African dance and marked a departure from the European style of dancing in couples.

It took years to capture the true excitement of dance on film. In 1933, two films paved the way for the following 20 years, which came to be known as the **Golden Era:** *42nd Street* with the wild cinematic choreography of Busby Berkeley and *Flying Down to Rio* with the subtle artistry of Fred Astaire, the most graceful and beguiling dancer the movies has ever known.

Busby Berkeley never studied dance or took a lesson, yet he was known for his endless ideas for dance routines. Berkeley was one of the top four dance directors on Broadway. His routines were characterized by intricate patterns created by groups of dancers. Ingenious camera movements and overhead camera projections made the patterns look as though they were a stop-frame kaleidoscope art. A string of major dance musicals fell under his direction: *42nd Street, Gold Diggers of 1933, 1935 and 1937,* and the Rooney–Garland musicals *Babes in Arms, Strike Up the Band,* and *Babes on Broadway.* Before his retirement in the early 1970s, Berkeley supervised the dance sequences of the Broadway smash *No, No, Nannette.* Berkeley's contribution to film meant the movie musical would never look the same again.

Although Astaire had been a vital part of Broadway throughout the 1920s, when musicals finally found their ground in Hollywood in 1933, he became *the* leading man for movie musicals. Astaire created a unique dance style that brought elegance to the dancer's image. He blended the flowing steps of ballet with the abruptness of jazz movements and was the first dancer to dance every musical note so that the rhythmic pattern of the music was mirrored in the dance steps.

Audiences were also intrigued by the sight of Astaire and Ginger Rogers in their complex dance duets. They were partners in a string of dance musical hits that included *Roberta* (1935), *Top Hat* (1935), *Follow the Fleet* (1936), *Swing Time* (1936), *Shall We Dance* (1937), *Carefree* (1938), and *The Story of Vernon and Irene Castle* (1939).

Over the next two decades after the split with Rogers, Astaire continued to dazzle audiences with his charismatic style of dancing with a list of stars — Leslie Caron, Cyd Charisse, Vera-Ellen, Judy Garland, and Jane Powell, to name a few. He also teamed up with male partners Bing Crosby and Gene Kelly. In 1949, when Judy Garland became ill during the making of *The Barkleys of Broadway,* MGM reunited Astaire and Rogers for their final appearance together.

In 1959, after a brief retirement, Astaire returned to dancing with a television video hour called "An Evening with Astaire," which was fol-

The jitterbug at a 1930s dance hall. Improvisation was the key to its excitement. Photo from New York Public Library at Lincoln Center.

The charismatic Fred Astaire, showing noncha- lance and sophistication. Photo from New York Public Library at Lincoln Center.

lowed in 1960 with "Another Evening with Astaire" and in 1961 with "Astaire Time." In 1981, much of Hollywood's royalty attended the gala televised gathering in which Astaire was awarded the American Film In- stitute's Lifetime Achievement Award.

For the audiences who grew up watching Fred Astaire and Ginger Rogers musicals, the moments of them together on film were magical. Although Rogers was criticized for having limited technique, her dancing was impeccable. She matched Astaire step for step. Rogers once said, "I did everything Fred did except backwards and in high heels." Rogers was the bridge between the uninhibited flappers of the 1920s and the well- trained dancers such as Cyd Charisse and Leslie Caron who appeared with Fred Astaire in the 1950s.

Cyd Charisse was one of the many Astaire dance partners to follow Ginger Rogers's footsteps. Charisse danced with ballet companies from the age of 14 under a variety of names. Her now-famous name was established when she did an opening dance sequence with Astaire in *Ziegfeld Follies* (1946). In her early career, Charisse danced with such famous names as Gower Champion, Ricardo Montalban, and Gene Kelly in *Singin' in the Rain*. *The Band Wagon* gave Charisse her first starring role, dancing with Fred Astaire to the choreography of Michael Kidd. In 1954 and 1955, Charisse again danced with Kelly in *Brigadoon* and *Always Fair Weather*. In 1957, she danced for a final time with Astaire in *Silk Stockings*. Although her career continued with a variety of performances both live and on film, the premiere compliment of her success was from Fred Astaire: "That Cyd! When you've danced with her you stay danced with."

Dance became further integrated into musical theater in 1936 with the Broadway production *On Your Toes,* choreographed by George Balanchine. *On Your Toes* is famous for its ballet centerpiece, "Slaughter on Tenth Avenue." Ray Bolger, with a comic flair, dances himself into a state of exhaustion in an attempt to elude capture by the gangster mob.

*T*HE 1940S

Just when social jazz dance was at its height, World War II put a stop to its popularity. Young men were enlisted to serve in battle while young women assisted the war effort in factories. Lack of attendance plus the intricate rhythmic patterns of modern jazz music, which were too complex for social dancing, led to the closing of dance halls and ballrooms. With the demise of social jazz dancing, the growth of jazz dance as a professional dance form began. During the 1940s, jazz dance was influenced by ballet and modern dance. By blending the classical technique of ballet with the natural bodily expression of modern dance, jazz dance developed a sophisticated and artistic quality. Unlike early jazz dance, which was performed by talented entertainers without formal training, modern jazz dance was performed by professionals trained in ballet and modern dance. It was at this time that jazz dance as we know it today made its claim on the Broadway stage and gained the respect of ballet and modern dance choreographers.

In 1943, *Oklahoma,* choreographed by Agnes de Mille, marked the beginning of dance as a major aspect of musical comedy. In the years that followed, other ballet choreographers became involved in Broadway musicals. Dance sequences in *On the Town* (1944) and in the ballet *Fancy Free* (1944), choreographed by Jerome Robbins, incorporated the newer, freer, and more rhythmic form of dance called jazz.

As jazz dance made its mark on the Broadway stage, its popularity in film continued. Gene Kelly began his movie career 10 years after Astaire established himself in Hollywood musicals. Although Kelly missed out on

Jerome Robbins's Fancy Free *with ballet star Fernando Bujones. Photo by Martha Swope.*

the heyday of movie musicals, he made an impact with his individual, energetic dance style that combined athletics, gymnastics, and dance.

Kelly's success in the Broadway hit *Pal Joey* (1940) was his vehicle to Hollywood and his movie debut in *For Me and My Gal*. His extensive list of film credits includes *Anchors Away* (1945) in which Kelly combined live action with cartoon animation. In *Words and Music* (1948), with its amazing "Slaughter on Tenth Avenue," Kelly rechoreographed Balanchine's ballet, shortening it from 11 to 7 minutes. *On the Town* (1949) became an important film musical, as it was the first to be filmed with extended sequences on location, using the city as a set and paving the way for musicals such as *West Side Story*. Among Kelly's impressive list of films are *An American in Paris* (1951) with the famous dream ballet finale, and *Singin' in the Rain* (1952), which some connoisseurs consider the best movie musical.

Kelly's career spanned the next two decades with a combination of dancing, choreography, and directing. In *That's Entertainment, Part II,* Kelly (age 64) and Astaire (age 70) proved that they could still dance with youthful agility. Kelly also contributed to the world of dance with the television special for Omnibus, *Dancing—A Man's Game* (1958), which was devised to educate the public and remove the stigma attached to male dancers. In 1983, Kelly became an honoree of the Kennedy Center in Washington, D.C.

Dance stars became popular during the 1940s. Some stars humorously called themselves "hoofers" (those who concentrate on the feet, without making hand and body movements); others considered themselves serious dancers. Whatever title they chose, numerous stars were popularized because of their dancing ability: Betty Grable, June Allyson, Dan Dailey, Mickey Rooney, Shirley Temple, Judy Garland, James Cagney, Rita Hayworth, and the remarkable Jack Cole.

Jack Cole, trained in modern dance, is often considered the father of jazz dance technique. With the increased demand for jazz dance in film and on the stage, it became necessary to develop a more serious and defined approach to jazz dance. Cole developed an innovative style and training technique that involved isolation of body parts, with natural body movements that flow from one action to the next. Besides his work as an innovator of jazz dance technique, Cole choreographed for films and Broadway; his most famous productions are *Kismet* (1953) and *Man of La Mancha* (1966).

Also at this time, Afro-Haitian, West Indian, and Latin dance forms fused with jazz dance, rejuvenating the primitive and earthy style of early jazz dance movements and incorporating a rhythmic drumbeat as the primary source of music. Katherine Dunham and Pearl Primus, two black dancers involved in the study of anthropology, researched these dance forms and contributed their findings to the growing vocabulary of modern jazz dance. Their work created a new respect for the ethnic beginnings of jazz dance.

THE 1950S

The decade opened with a new attitude: The public wanted musicals with serious themes. More than any other musical produced in the early 1950s, *Guys and Dolls* epitomized the new stature of American musical comedy as a form of dramatic art. Every song, dance, and line of dialogue developed the plot.

Other notable examples of the fusion of dance and drama in film are *An American in Paris* (1951) and *Singin' in the Rain* (1952), both choreographed by Gene Kelly. Michael Kidd is also among the outstanding names of those who produced motion picture choreography in which

Katherine Dunham rekindled interest in the ethnic origins of jazz dance. Photo from New York Public Library at Lincoln Center.

dance furthers the story line. His dance expertise is well noted in *It's Always Fair Weather* (1955) starring Gene Kelly. His film work includes such superb titles as *Where's Charley?* (1952), *The Bandwagon* (1953), *Seven Brides for Seven Brothers* (1954), *Guys and Dolls, Li'l Abner,* and *Hello, Dolly!* (1969).

Debbie Reynolds was another familiar name in movie musicals of the 1950s. Although not a trained dancer, Reynolds possessed a stage charisma that was backed by unrelenting enthusiasm. Her breakthrough in 1950 was in *Two Weeks with Love* starring Jane Powell and Ricardo Montalban. Because of this success, Gene Kelly chose her to star with him in *Singin' in the Rain*. In 1953, she choreographed and danced in *Give a Girl a Break* with Gower Champion. Also in 1953, she starred opposite

The exciting jazz ballet from West Side Story, *choreographed by Jerome Robbins. Photo by Martha Swope.*

Donald O'Conner in *I Love Melvin*. Over the years, Reynolds continued her career on stage and as a top Las Vegas entertainer. Her training studio in Hollywood today is a major site for professional auditions.

As the decade continued, dance became an important element in characterization as well. In *West Side Story* (1957), choreographer Jerome Robbins thrilled audiences by using jazz dance to show the brutality and bravado of warring street gangs and the exuberance of Latin culture. Robbins adapted a step from the Black Bottom to capture the style of west side ghetto kids. The new move, called the pimp walk, is unmistakable: The dancer leans forward at the waist, shoulders and knees high, and snaps his fingers.

Matt Mattox views the body as a straight line and then sees what designs can come from it. Photo from New York Public Library at Lincoln Center.

Social dance had suffered a decline in the early 1950s. Perhaps, with the Korean War, McCarthyism, and the hydrogen bomb, Americans had little to dance about. But by 1955, youngsters were beginning to dance to a new musical style: rock and roll. Rock and roll was a re-creation by white musicians of the kind of music black musicians had been performing for 50 years. Teenagers now danced in their homes and at record hops to popular music that had a big and often monotonous offbeat.

In 1956, Elvis Presley arrived from the South as a new teen idol, and he transformed the sound of rock and roll. Presley presented a blend of hillbilly, gospel, blues, and popular music and introduced his sound to TV audiences. As the enthusiasm for rock and roll music continued, dancing increased, accelerated by Dick Clark's television program "American Bandstand." In the foreground was a group of authentically awkward young dancers with whom any teenager could identify; in the background groups sang lip-sync to their own recordings. A wave of new group dances became popular: the Madison, the Birdland, the Bop, the Locomotion, the Chicken, and the Mashed Potato. Surprisingly, however, many of these dances were throwbacks to earlier eras. The Chicken was a parody of the Lindy-Hop; the Mashed Potato was reminiscent of the Charleston.

During this period, Matt Mattox emerged as a major talent in the development of professional jazz dance. Mattox's technique involves the isolation of body parts and the view that the body, in its simplest form, is a straight line from which designs can be created. (Mattox may have developed the straight-line idea from Jack Cole's study of the linear design of East Indian dance.) The Mattox style is percussive, with strong angular movements and sharp accents, rebounds, and turns. Mattox choreographed for Broadway, television, and ballet companies.

THE 1960S The early 1960s introduced the Twist. The Twist, characterized by Presley- like hip gyrations, partners never touching but responding to each other's movements, brought adults back to the social dance floor. The Twist became an overnight craze because it was so easy to perform.

While adults twisted with Chubby Checker, the 1960s teenagers were ready for a new movement and a new sound. Out of Detroit came a new musical revolution: Motown. Motown groups featured a chorus that performed choreographed routines while the lead singer was spotlighted in the forefront. On the dance floor teens copied the choruses by performing line dances. The most popular was the Stroll, which reemerged in later years as the Hustle.

The innovative and danceable music of the Beatles rocked American culture like an explosion. The teenage population especially was attracted to the dance floor by the immense popularity of the Beatles' music, which incorporated a variety of rhythms and interesting, relevant lyrics. Following in the wave of success of the Beatles were a flood of look-alike, sound-alike musical groups that gave social dance yet another boost.

The youth of America found another style of dance expression in the popular depictions of California. TV offered "77 Sunset Strip," and Hollywood cranked out an endless stream of beach blanket movies. The music reflected the craze with songs by the Ventures, Surfaris, Jan and Dean, and the Beach Boys. A whole new wave of dances emerged: the Swim, the Jerk, the Monkey, and the Hitchhiker. The explosion gave social dance yet another boost. By 1965 there were 5,000 discotheques in America. Dance studios flourished as dance enthusiasts attempted to keep abreast of dance fads that came and went from week to week.

The hippie, "flower child," years of the late 1960s brought a new style of rock music influenced by psychedelic drugs and political protest, and a revival of old dance halls—now the scene of live rock music, psychedelic light shows, and solo improvisatory dancing.

More and more television shows featured music and professional dancing. Most notable were "Shindig," "Hullabaloo," and "Laugh-In." Hosts of other TV variety shows—Dean Martin, Jackie Gleason, and Ed Sullivan—often featured a line of dancers as backup for a star performer. Television thus helped to popularize dance crazes while giving dancers a steady income. As the alternatives for a dance career increased, so did the need for formal training.

During the 1960s, two major names appeared among the ranks of professional jazz dance greats: Eugene Louis Facciuto—or Luigi, as he

The Gus Giordano Jazz Dance Chicago troupe. Giordano's technique is influenced by the natural and free body movements of modern dance. Photo by John Randolph.

is called—and Gus Giordano. Both men achieved continuing fame as developers of jazz dance technique and choreography.

Luigi developed his technique as a result of an auto accident that left him paralyzed on the right side. Doctors claimed he would never walk, let alone dance again. But Luigi persisted with operations, physical therapy, and his own study of body development based on dance exercise. He attained the ability to move and dance again, and he began to teach the technique he had learned. Luigi taught a series of exercises that used the total body in each movement phase. His technique requires that the body be exercised to its fullest to develop the strength necessary for muscle control, yet still look beautiful. The Luigi technique, influenced by ballet training, is lyrical. It is best described in his own book, *Jazz with Luigi.*

Gus Giordano's style is classical, but it is greatly influenced by the natural and freer body movements of modern dance. His technique teaches isolation movements, emphasizing the head and torso and creating an up-lifted look of elegance. Yoga is incorporated into his technique as a means of relaxation. Further study of Gus Giordano might be made through his book, *Anthology of American Jazz Dance.*

Although the focus of the 1960s seemed to be on the revolution of musical change and social dance innovations, jazz dance maintained a respectable position on the Broadway stage. Notable jazz dance productions of this decade were *Cabaret,* choreographed by Ron Field, and *Sweet Charity,* choreographed by Bob Fosse.

THE 1970S

In the 1970s, the public was more receptive to a broad variety of entertainment forms, as can be seen in the wide range of musical styles that appeared at this time. College students attended rock concerts, aspiring musicians played free concerts in city parks, and folk music was heard in restaurant lounges. Musical tastes ranged from acid rock to electronic music to soul and lyrical jazz. Discotheques (now called discos) gave rise to such choreographed line dances as the Bus Stop, the Roller Coaster, and the Hustle. The Bump, another popular dance, encouraged bodily contact as partners bumped one another with various parts of their anatomies.

A notable jazz dance production of the 1970s was *Grease,* a nostalgic re-creation of teenage life in the 1950s, featuring the era's enthusiastic dances to high-energy rock and roll tunes. At the theater, the public fell in love with Michael Bennett's *A Chorus Line* (1975). Dance as the primary theme of a production was now able to capture the attention of a Broadway crowd.

John Travolta made the decade's biggest impact on dancing in the movie *Saturday Night Fever* (1977), which became a box office smash. With his lead role in *Saturday Night Fever* came instant stardom. To prepare for his role, Travolta visited many New York discos. He also ran two hours a day and danced three hours a day to get in shape for the dancing. In the 1980s movie sequel, *Stayin' Alive,* Travolta appears again as a male dancer, this time auditioning and performing in a Broadway production in the movie's storyline. Charismatic, sexy, and very physical in his dance movements, Travolta boosts the image of male dancers.

In the 1970s, Bob Fosse became the outstanding name in jazz dance. Although he worked as a performer on Broadway and in films, Fosse's true success was as a choreographer, beginning with his first choreography, *Pajama Game,* in 1954, and followed by *Damn Yankees* (1955), *Bells Are Ringing* (1956), *New Girl in Town* (1957), *Redhead* (1959), *Little Me* (1962), *Sweet Charity* (1967), and *Chicago* (1975). In 1973, Fosse was the first director in history to win three national entertainment awards: the Oscar for his film version of *Caberet,* the Tony for the Broadway musical *Pippin,* and the Emmy for the television special *Liza with a Z.* In 1978, Fosse received a second Tony award for his Broadway success *Dancin'.* Drawing on his varied talents, Fosse also directed, co-authored, and choreographed the widely acclaimed and Oscar-nominated film *All That Jazz* (1979).

Fosse's style was distinct. It was highly creative and often included bizarre movements. Hiw choreography was slick, erotic, and intense. There were many poses characteristic of the Fosse style; most recognizable was the long-legged look with raised arm and limp wrist. Fosse and his highly personalized jazz dance style continued to make a mark on the

Bob Fosse's Tony award-winning show Dancin'. *Fosse's dances are slick and entertaining. Photo by Martha Swope.*

Broadway stage and in Hollywood films throughout the 1980s. Fosse was a one-man jazz phenomenon.

Another important 1970s influence on jazz dance came not from a person, but from an area. Out of the ghetto neighborhoods of New York City came a new dance phenomenon called breakdancing. **Breakdancing** is a generic term for all forms of modern street dance. These forms include breaking (specific moves done on or close to the floor—spins, windmills, 1990s, swipes, and footwork), freestyle (gymnastic movements and disco partner lifts), electric boogie (flowing movements that enter through one body part and exit through another), popping (any staccato movement), Egyptian (an imitation of Egyptian-style art), and floating (steps such as the moonwalk, in which the feet seem to float across the floor). Most often, a breakdancer combines a variety of these styles to complete a breakdance routine.

Where did this dancing style come from? Just as the roots of jazz dance are African, breakdancing can be traced to the West African cultures of Mali, Gambia, and Senegal. In the late 1960s, many West African dancers came to America and settled in the South Bronx. Breakdancing emerged, not as an entertainment form, but as a competition. Skill in breakdancing was a means of attaining superiority in street-corner fraternities; it was an alternative to gang warfare. In the 1980s, breakdancing exploded out of the ghettos and into mainstream American dance culture.

Jazz dance further expanded its horizons when it combined with physical fitness classes to make exercise more fun and sociable. The result was a new hybrid: aerobic dance classes. The popularity of the combination of dance and aerobic exercise has created such great interest that over 20 million people now participate in this form of exercise.

THE 1980S

The most prominent name in 1980s musical theater was Andrew Lloyd Webber, who is acclaimed for shifting the focus of the Broadway musical from America to the London stage. His musical hits include *Jesus Christ Superstar, Joseph and the Amazing Technicolor Dreamcoat, Starlight Express, Phantom of the Opera,* and the hottest musical of the 1980s, *Cats.* In *Cats,* dancers portrayed felines with distinct characters and danced with the litheness and agility of their feline counterparts. The choreography of Gillian Lynne was a primary means of characterization, and she earned several major awards for her outstanding work.

The movies of the 1980s gave jazz dance a tremendous boost. Two of the most prominent movies of the decade were *Fame* (1980) and *Flashdance* (1983). In *Fame,* high school students danced in their professional preparation classes, in their classrooms, in the cafeteria, and down the streets. There was no end to the energy and talent, not only of the students, but of the teachers as well. Debbie Allen, portraying the dance instructor, amazed the audience with her talent and innovative choreography. Hollywood noticed the popularity of this film, and soon *Fame* became a weekly television program highlighted by at least one major dance presentation in each episode. Adolescents were inspired by the achievements of these youths and joined jazz dance classes in hope of attaining their own fame. In *Flashdance,* the characters realized their dreams of success through a story line dominated by dance performances. Other dance films that drew audiences to the movies included *Stayin' Alive* (1983), *Footloose* (1984), *Breakdancing* (1985), and *Dirty Dancing* (1987). Although these films lacked a strong story line, showy jazz dance sequences appealed to a wide audience. Dance studios and jazz dance classes were crowded with eager students interested in conquering this exciting dance form.

That's Dancin' (1986) outlines the history of dance, including a brief

Radio City Rockettes take a basic jazz position in their chorus line pose.
Photo by Martha Swope.

introduction on dance as a part of early human development. Depictions of dance appear in cave art, sculpture, and drawings. Narrator Gene Kelly traces the origins of today's modern dance to the late 1800s, when the motion picture camera was first invented. Kelly leads the audience through decades of dance on film. *That's Dancin'* is an entertaining, educational dance film that appeals to young and old alike.

American business noticed the large audience appeal of jazz dance and quickly moved to capitalize on the craze. As never before, jazz dance appeared in television commercials: Panasonic, Coca-Cola, and several major fast-food chains featured dance as a selling aspect for their products.

A new medium for dance and professional dancers in the 1980s was the music video. When MTV began broadcasting in 1981, music videos combined high-energy jazz, ballet, street dance, and social dance in striking, innovative ways. Over 130 million people see MTV clips each day, and the choreographers' names—Michael Peters, Jeffery Hornaday, Lester Wilson, Toni Basil, Paula Abdul, Madonna, Janet Jackson, and

*Michael Jackson in his
music video "Billy
Jean." Photo by
AP/Wide World Photos.*

others—have become household words. One name, however, stands su-
preme among the video stars of the 1980s—Michael Jackson.

Michael Jackson, the youngest member of The Jackson Five from the
Motown era, was singing and dancing his way to stardom. His talent for
both song and dance provided a natural transition to MTV production.
Jackson made a major impact on the direction of jazz dance with his creative and imaginative dance steps and choreography. His style was well
marked with personalized movements and poses: his sexy sit pose and
wide knock-kneed position; his fast jumping-jack foot action with a quick
crossed foot turn; his famous pencil spin that revolved like a spinning top;
his head, shoulder, and rib isolations and erotic and suggestive hip

thrusts; the moonwalk; and his trademark toe rise. In his earlier video productions, "Don't Stop 'til You Get Enough" and "Rock with You" (both 1979), the music retained the sound of the decade's disco beat, and the format was relatively simple with a few lighting and technical effects. In the early 1980s, however, Jackson exploded on the video screen with elaborate and intricate technical productions. In 1982, he dominated the screen with "Thriller," "Beat It," and "Billie Jean." In 1987, "The Way You Make Me Feel" and "Bad" took command of both the music and video charts across the country. Jackson was not just an American success; he was an international star. His elaborate productions and distinctive trademarks, such as the single glove, set him apart as a performer. Much of Jackson's choreography was created by Michael Peters or by Peters and Jackson collaborating as a team. Jackson's impact on jazz dance—his music, his videos, his choreography, his style, and his presentation—is almost immeasurable.

In the 1980s, another name was added to the list of professional instructors who have influenced the development of jazz dance—Joe Tremaine. In the early 1960s, he arrived in the Big Apple to study ballet with Vencinzo Celli, the techniques of modern jazz and the isolation of body parts with Matt Mattox, lyrical jazz technique from Luigi, and the fusion of jazz and modern dance from Claude Thompson. Tremaine's early experiences included "The Jackie Gleason Show," weekly television variety shows, television specials, and a European series under the direction of Nick Castle who, impressed by Tremaine's performances, asked him to work on "The Jerry Lewis Show" as the lead dancer. His performance on "The Jerry Lewis Show" was seen by Eugene Loring, choreographer of ballets such as *Billy the Kid,* who offered him a teaching position at his American School of Dance.

Tremaine is a natural teacher; his teaching style is comparable to his style on the dance floor—up to the minute, fast, flashy, and funky. The variety of techniques he brought from New York are also a part of Tremaine's unique style, which many refer to as "West Coast jazz" or "L.A. jazz." Tremaine's style, driven by current musical trends, is rhythmical and jazzy. When Gus Giordano organized the First American Jazz Dance World Congress, he invited jazz legends Luigi and Matt Mattox. The East Coast was represented by Frank Hatchett and the West Coast by Joe Tremaine. Tremaine received the American Video Conference Award for the "Best Dance Instruction Video" (1988), the "Gus Giordano Dance Award" (1990), and the "Dance Educators of America Award (1992). He has taught, coached, or choreographed for a long list of stars including Paula Abdul, Ann-Margret, Liza Minelli, and Debbie Reynolds. Despite the allure of Hollywood glamour and awards, Tremaine's passion remains in teaching.

At his Hollywood studio, Tremaine teaches a challenging schedule of classes from beginner to advanced. Over the years, he has developed professional dancers and choreographers.

Tremaine has channeled his enthusiasm for dance in yet another direction—his own dance conventions and competitions. Through his conventions and competitions, Tremaine brings his Hollywood style to nearly 30,000 dancers a year. The popularity of Tremaine conventions has affected the dance history of the 1990s. His dream is to expand his conventions internationally, bringing his fast, funky style of jazz to other countries.

THE 1990S

The 1990s has maintained the status quo in shows, films, and innovations from the late 1980s. Andrew Lloyd Webber continues to be the key name in musical theater with the ongoing success of the shows he created in the 1980s. Very little has been done in film featuring jazz dance. Unfortunately, the dance world has lost many talented choreographers and dancers to the AIDS epidemic. As a result, the hottest tickets on Broadway are reproductions from past decades such as *Guys and Dolls, Crazy for You, Showboat, Damn Yankees,* and *Tommy.* The 1990s is an era in which the best of Broadway past reigns.

One new name that has emerged, however, is that of choreographer and dancer Tommy Tune. In 1969, he appeared in *Hello, Dolly!* starring Barbra Streisand, and he was prominent in *The Boyfriend* (1971). Tune has since established himself as a vital dancer and choreographer. He has toured with a one-man show that highlights his dancing elegance, and he choreographed *Will Rogers' Follies* (1993).

In the 1990s jazz dance world, the buzz words in training centers are *street dancing, street funk,* and *hip hop.* Street dancing is inner-city dance taken directly from the streets. It is a freestyle form of dance done on the street corners with performers using "boom" boxes to play accompanying music. The "Fly Girls," dancers featured between comedy skits on Fox's early '90s TV hit, *In Living Color,* gave many prime-time viewers their first look at street dance. *Street dancing* may be considered an umbrella term that encompasses funk, popping, breakdancing, and hip hop.

Hip hop, a style from the streets, has gained in popularity as its freestyle movements and fast footwork are incorporated into social dance via clubs. Hip hop moves to a syncopated beat—a rhythmic shuffle beat. The style of the movements are bouncy, fast, and funky. Hip hop uses the whole body but is primarily foot oriented. To give the emphasized footwork complexity, upper-body movements and isolations are incorporated. Hip hop is a raw form of dance that is also trick oriented in its use of breakdancing and gymnastic moves. The total freedom of its movements allows the dancer to improvise.

Hip hop is a style of clothing, attitude, and music. Hip hop music has evolved through the rap music culture. Originally, hip hop music had only rapping but now has rapping and/or singing to the beat, which makes it more versatile.

Hip hop and other new street funk movements generally originate in either New York or Los Angeles. MTV is the main vehicle that introduces these steps to the rest of America. Dancers have the need to be acutely aware of the latest steps and styles. As a result, dance training centers are filling classes with dancers mastering this highly energetic and currently popular trend of jazz dance.

The jazz dance performance world has taken a few new turns in the 1990s. Professional jazz dance has sought a new and wider variety of performance platforms including cabaret and lounge shows, cruise ship entertainment, and touring dance companies. Concert tours with musical superstars feature dancers as an integral part of their concert entertainment. Jazz dance, and in particular musical comedy, has become primary in theme park entertainment. Music videos still prominently use jazz dance. Major television productions such as award presentation galas continue to feature jazz dance. Industrials—promotional business shows—use jazz dance as a feature in sales promotion and display of their products.

Jazz dance has also expanded its parameters from being solely a creative and entertaining experience to becoming a competitive event. Jazz dance has embraced America's youth, and young people are responding with overwhelming enthusiasm. Dance schools are integrating dance competition as a part of students' training and development. Major dance conventions and competitions are featured across the nation with age group divisions ranging from preschool to adult. Awards are presented for dance and choreography, and studios also receive recognition. The ultimate experience for the dancer is to compete in television events that involve international competition and substantial monetary reward. Most prized in winning, however, is the possibility of being recognized by one of the Hollywood talent agencies that offer contracts to up-and-coming talent. Because of its emphasis on competition and athleticism, it's not unthinkable that jazz dance may become an Olympic event.

The history of jazz dance has evolved in pace with the music and the moods of each decade (see Table 1-1). Jazz dance gives way to rules and restrictions and allows for its art form to be versatile, spontaneous, contemporary, and exciting. Now it's time for you to take the step to be a part of the making of jazz dance history and *Jump into Jazz!*

TABLE I-I JAZZ DANCE HISTORY AT A GLANCE

	PEOPLE	DANCES	SHOWS	INNOVATIONS AND EVENTS
1800s		Cakewalk	Minstrel shows	Fugitive Slave Act of 1859
1900		The buck-and-wing	Vaudeville	
1910	Vernon and Irene Castle	One-step dances Castlewalk Foxtrot		World War I
1920s	Josephine Baker Bill "Bojangles" Robinson	Charleston	*Shuffle Along* *Runnin' Wild*	Dixieland Jazz Talkies
1930s	Duke Ellington Louis Armstrong Busby Berkeley Fred Astaire Ginger Rogers George Balanchine	Jitterbug Boogie-woogie Lindy-Hop	*42nd Street* *Flying Down to Rio* *On Your Toes*	Big bands Savoy Ballroom The Depression Dance marathons
1940s	Agnes de Mille Jerome Robbins Gene Kelly Jack Cole Katherine Dunham		*Oklahoma* *On The Town* *Fancy Free* *Pal Joey* *Anchors Away*	World War II
1950s	Michael Kidd Matt Mattox Elvis Presley Cyd Charisse Debbie Reynolds	Rock and roll Rock and roll group dances The Madison The Birdland The Bop Locomotion Mashed Potato The Chicken	*An American in Paris* *Seven Brides for Seven Brothers* *Guys and Dolls* *Singin' in the Rain* *West Side Story*	Korean War Pimp walk Rock and roll music American Bandstand
1960s	Chubby Checker The Beatles Luigi Gus Giordano	The Twist Line dances The Stroll The Hustle	*Cabaret* *Sweet Charity*	Motown TV variety shows featuring dance Discotheques Psychedelic era Hippies

TABLE 1-1 JAZZ DANCE HISTORY AT A GLANCE

	PEOPLE	DANCES	SHOWS	INNOVATIONS AND EVENTS
1970s	Michael Bennett Bob Fosse John Travolta	Disco dance Breakdancing	*Grease* *A Chorus Line* *Cabaret* (film) *Pippin* *All That Jazz* *Dancin'* *Saturday Night Fever*	Aerobic dance
1980s	Andrew Lloyd Webber Michael Jackson Joe Tremaine	The moonwalk Funk	*Cats* *Fame* *Flashdance* *That's Dancin'*	MTV "Thriller" "Beat It" "Billie Jean"
1990s	Tommy Tune	Street Funk Hip hop	*Guys and Dolls* *Crazy for You* *Tommy* *Showboat* *Damn Yankees*	Dance competitions

Frank Hatchett, New York jazz dance teacher and choreographer, demonstrates that jazz dance can start at an early age.

CHAPTER 2

GETTING STARTED

Most students enrolled in a jazz dance class for the first time need information about what to wear and how to present themselves in class. Although specific requirements vary, there are some basic conventions in dress, appearance, and etiquette that the student should know. This chapter discusses these common conventions and also outlines the basic structure of a jazz dance lesson.

ATTIRE

Dance is perceived as a series of designs in space, created through body positions and movements. It is therefore essential that dance clothing reveal body line and allow freedom of movement.

The primary focus of the beginning jazz dance student is the imitation of the instructor's positions and movements, with special attention given to body alignment and placement (see Chapter 3, "A Dancer's Alignment"). Wearing the proper clothing will enable your instructor to check your body line and will help you check yourself in the studio mirror.

Clothing

Women generally wear a leotard and tights. The tights come in a variety of lengths, from fully footed to very short "hot pants." Tights can be worn under or over the leotard, depending on taste and style. Underwear is generally not worn beneath the tights because its outline shows below the line of the leotard and disrupts the long, smooth look of the leg.

Support undergarments are extremely important for the dancer. Women should wear a bra that fits snugly and supplies adequate support for jumping movements. Specific dance or sports bras can be purchased in many retail stores as well as dance attire stores.

The more traditional men's dance attire also consists of leotard and tights. The tights are heavier material than that of the women's tights, yet they also come in a variety of lengths. A dance belt is worn under the tights and serves the same purpose as an athletic supporter. The dance belt gives more support, however, because it is constructed for the variety of stretching, jumping, and leg-lifting activities performed in dance.

Although men wear leotards in styles cut for the male body, they wear their tights over the leotards. The tights are held up either by a belt or an elastic around the waist, over which the tights are rolled, or by clip-on suspenders.

With the rising popularity of dancewear and exercise attire as street clothing, the variety of styles, fabrics, and colors is greater than it has ever been. Both men and women wear unitards, jazz pants, bicycle shorts, and leotard half-tops designed in either Lycra or cotton blend. In addition to the essential items of dress, dancers often wear leg or ankle warmers, sweatpants or pants or shorts of rip-stop nylon, sweater pants, sweater tops, or sweatshirts. (Because muscles perform best when warm, these accessories accelerate the rise in body heat during the warm-up period or initial class activities.) Some teachers may not approve of sweatpants as part of the attire, since they hide the line of the body and therefore, corrections on technique cannot be easily made.

In most jazz dance classes students are free to create their own clothing ensembles. However, ask the instructor about the dress code before making dance attire purchases.

Dance Footwear

Depending on the type of dance studio floor, shoes may or may not be required. If shoes are worn in class, students may want to try the leather or canvas jazz shoe, the jazz sandal, or the suede-strapped sandal shoe.

Jazz shoes can be purchased at most dance supply stores. Several shoe companies make the jazz shoe, which comes in a variety of styles. The typical shoe is a soft leather and is available in a low-top or high-top (jazz boot) style. The sole of the shoe is either a full sole or a "split sole," where a break in the sole allows for more foot flexibility. The split sole makes pointing the foot easier. The high-top jazz shoe is usually more expensive but is becoming very popular because it provides additional support for the ankle. The slip-on version of the jazz shoe is another popular style. It is optimal because it is easy to put on and because its smooth line accentuates the pointed foot. The least expensive shoe is a canvas low-top shoe, but unfortunately this shoe is stiff and therefore the point of the foot is harder to see. A picture of the typical jazz shoe is illustrated in Figure 2-1.

Some instructors may also allow ballet or gymnastic shoes. The ballet shoe is shown in Figure 2-2.

FIGURE 2-1 Jazz shoe

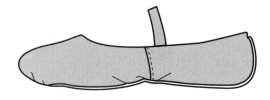

FIGURE 2-2 Ballet shoe

"Character shoes" (shoes with 2-inch heels) are often worn by women for auditions or performances but are not usually recommended for lessons.

APPEARANCE

Good grooming habits are as essential for the dance classroom as they are in daily life. The hair should be secured away from the face so that it is not bothersome. Excessive jewelry should not be worn, for it distracts from the body line and can disrupt dance movements or injure other dancers. Elastic straps to secure eyeglasses in place are encouraged. If a student perspires heavily, it is appropriate to bring a small towel to use during lesson breaks.

ETIQUETTE

The basic rules of etiquette for the dance classroom promote consideration for other dancers and allow the class to proceed smoothly and rapidly, without interruption and delay. The student should arrive on time or early for the dance lesson. Arriving late not only is rude to the instructor, but also is harmful to the dancer, for it hurries the body into vigorous exercise without a proper warm-up. The result may be serious injury. Some instructors do not allow a student to enter the classroom after a determined point in the initial activities or a determined time after the lesson starts.

At no time should a student enter a classroom with food, drink, or chewing gum. Considerate students do not talk unnecessarily or interrupt the instructor during the instruction period. Most teachers will ask for questions at appropriate intervals.

When locomotor movements or dance combinations are performed across the floor, a line generally is formed at either one side or one corner of the room. Students move with a partner, in fours, or in a group number assigned by the teacher. As you approach the front of the line, join your partner or group quickly and be ready to move at the start of your turn. Do not stop a dance combination midway across the floor, because the group of dancers immediately following you would be disrupted. When you complete your turn, etiquette prescribes that you walk around the perimeter of the room to return to the end of the line.

When dance combinations are to be performed in the center of the floor, stand in an area where the instructor is either directly visible or visible in the mirror. As the center dance combinations are performed, be aware of the movement space and do not intrude into the space of other students.

At the close of the dance lesson, students usually applaud in unison. This applause expresses appreciation both for the instruction the teacher has given and for the efforts and performances of fellow students.

TYPICAL STRUCTURE OF A JAZZ DANCE CLASS

Although all instructors have their own personal lesson formats, the following activities are characteristic of a jazz dance lesson.

Pre–Warm-Up

Many lessons begin with pre–warm-up exercises—very simple and slow body movements that align and prime the body for the warm-up exercises that follow. The pre–warm-up is also important for any dancer who has had a previous injury. The pre–warm-up is the time to focus on the injured body part so that it is prepared for the warm-up ahead.

Many teachers expect students to begin this part of the lesson on their own, which is why an early arrival to class is encouraged. Learn to assess your need for a pre–warm-up, and arrive early enough to complete the exercises before class.

Warm-Up

Warm-up exercises stimulate blood circulation to the muscles by progressive movements that gradually stretch, strengthen, align, and coordinate the body. Warm-up exercises are done in a variety of positions—standing, at the **barre,*** sitting, or lying on the floor. Included in the warm-up may be exercises for the development of basic dance technique. The warm-up may also introduce specific jazz movements that will later be incorporated into dance combinations. Isolation movements, an integral part of jazz dance, are often performed during the warm-up.

Isolation Exercises

Isolation exercises train the dancer to isolate and move each body part—such as the head, shoulders, rib cage, or hips—through its possible positions. Instructors sometimes combine various isolation movements so that two or more body parts move at the same time, thus helping the student develop coordination. Students may perform isolation exercises while standing or while moving across the floor.

Locomotor Movements

At the conclusion of the warm-up period, the student performs **locomotor movements,** or movement combinations, across the floor. This part of the lesson is usually the first opportunity for the student to perform dance steps. Locomotor movements stress the technical approach to dance steps and may introduce movement sequences that later will be presented in a dance combination.

Dance Combinations

In the jazz dance class, the culmination of the lesson is the learning and performing of a dance combination—a combination of movements using all the elements of dance and testing the dancer's technique, coordination, and memory.

    The instructor demonstrates the movement patterns of the dance combination in short sequences, explaining the counts, the spatial direction, and the proper techniques of executing specific steps. When the students have learned the dance steps and are able to execute the transitions from one movement to the next, the music for the performance of the combination is introduced. At this point, the class generally is divided into smaller groups that present the combination alternately. Students can learn from their own performances and also from watching other dancers perform. Students should observe carefully the flow of the move-

---

*****barre:** a long, horizontal wooden bar, attached to the wall or freestanding, used for support and balance.

ments, the transitions between steps, the exact positions of the body, the timing of intricate steps, and the style of performance.

Cool-Down

The cool-down is usually performed by students on their own: It is not often part of the format of a jazz dance class. A thorough cool-down helps prevent the dizziness and lightheadedness that could occur if a dancer quits vigorous activity abruptly. The cool-down also helps prevent muscle soreness.

How to Have a Successful Dance Class

Throughout the lesson, the instructor will give general corrections to the class as a whole and sometimes specific criticisms to individual students. Constructive criticism is offered to assist the student in learning the techniques of dance quickly and correctly. It is important to listen to any corrections, criticisms, or compliments the teacher gives, even if he or she is speaking to another student. These instructions may make you aware of techniques or draw your attention to areas in which you need to improve.

Dance students should practice outside of class, using the corrections given in lessons. Often there is a progression of dance steps and combinations from one class to the next. The student who practices the combinations outside class will experience the greatest and quickest progress.

Checklist for Success

1. Arrive at class 10 to 15 minutes early to give yourself a pre–warm-up.
2. Do not eat a heavy meal prior to class. A piece of fruit, yogurt, dried fruit, or nuts are recommended preclass snacks.
3. Come to class in the appropriate dance attire.
4. Clear your mind of outside interference when you enter the classroom. Be prepared to concentrate fully on the lesson.
5. Find a space to stand where you can see and hear the teacher. Allow yourself plenty of room so that you can move and stretch freely.
6. Be sensitive to any injuries you might have. Give special attention to the injured area during pre–warm-up exercises as well as in class activities. Do not overstretch or otherwise stress injured body parts.

7. If there is a review of combinations from class to class, mentally go over the steps before class so that you will be prepared either to perform the combination or to receive further choreographic instruction.

8. Do not be afraid to ask questions if you are unclear or want to improve your understanding of a certain technique.

9. Do not compare yourself to others in the class. However, learn to improve your performance by watching and imitating the more skilled dancers in the class.

10. Be aware of the ability level of the class in which you enroll. Do not take a class that is beyond your level—doing so can lead to frustration. On occasion, a more advanced class may be fun for a challenge.

11. Participate in dance class to improve your skill, knowledge, and aesthetic sense and to have a good time!

Break a leg!

A pose from the 1980s musical Cats, *music by Andrew Lloyd Webber and choreography by Gillian Lynn*

CHAPTER 3

A DANCER'S ALIGNMENT

Correct skeletal alignment is necessary for the jazz dancer. With correct alignment the dancer can achieve maximum balance and attain ease of movement whether standing, turning, jumping, or falling. Alignment is also the basis for effective movement patterns, helps to prevent injury, and creates the best body image. Because there are so many variations in body types, there is always disagreement on what "ideal posture" is. In this chapter, we analyze the body's alignment and attempt to define a body posture that is effective and efficient for all body types. We also discuss postural deviations and present exercises to help achieve efficient alignment.

POSTURE, BODY ALIGNMENT, AND PLACEMENT

Posture refers specifically to the position of the entire body in space. A person can take many different postures, yet he or she might not be properly aligned. **Alignment** refers specifically to the relationship of the individual body segments to each other. We look at the alignment of the spine in relationship to the head and legs. **Placement** is where the body is weighted in the space. You know from experience that, without visibly changing your position, you can shift your weight from the front of your foot to your heels. This weight shift is referred to as the placement of the body. Correct placement is critical for efficient and effective movement.

Posture, placement, and alignment are the basics of dance. Of these three, alignment is the most fundamental because it defines the dancer before movement begins. A misaligned dancer looks "wrong," even when posture and placement are correct. In addition, when the body is aligned, there is minimum strain on the muscles and ligaments attached to the weight-bearing joints. A misaligned dancer has a strong chance of becoming an injured dancer.

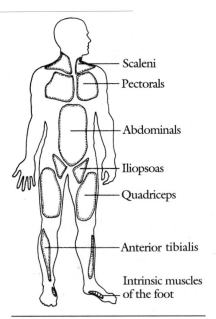

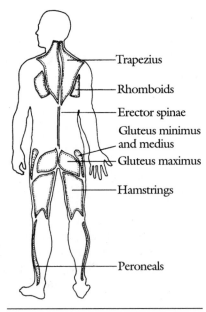

FIGURE 3-1 Muscles that hold the body erect, front view

FIGURE 3-2 Muscles that hold the body erect, rear view

Consider how the body maintains a vertical posture. Figures 3-1 and 3-2 show the major muscles involved in this job. The muscles must resist the force of gravity as well as the pull of the muscle that opposes it. The quadriceps, for example, are opposed by the hamstrings. Gravity tends to misalign the skeletal framework at three principal areas: the ankles, the knees, and the hips. An unbalanced relationship between opposing muscles in any part of the body can also cause misalignment.

*A*LIGNMENT REFERENCE POINTS

Basic body structure is, of course, determined by the skeleton. Figure 3-3 shows the major structural elements from the front. Figure 3-4 shows them from the back. Every individual's body structure is different, but there are visual guidelines for evaluating alignment. Figure 3-5 shows a side view of the body in correct alignment. The dotted line in the fig-

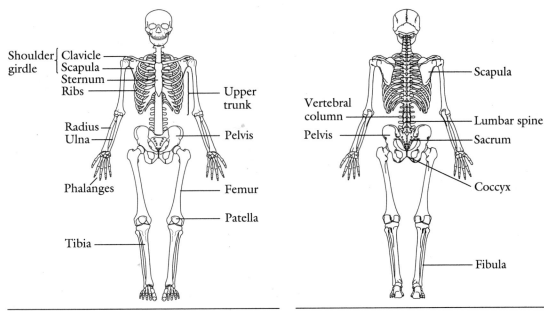

Shoulder ┤ Clavicle
girdle   └ Scapula
Sternum
Ribs
Upper trunk
Radius
Ulna
Pelvis
Phalanges
Femur
Patella
Tibia

FIGURE 3-3 Important skeletal structures, front view

Scapula
Vertebral column
Lumbar spine
Pelvis
Sacrum
Coccyx
Fibula

FIGURE 3-4 Important skeletal structures, rear view

ure represents the line of gravity, which pulls straight down on the body. In a correctly aligned body, the line passes through the specific points shown in the figure. These points, called alignment reference points, are as follows:

- The top of the ear
- The middle of the shoulder girdle
- The center of the hip
- The back of the kneecap
- The front of the anklebone

Figure 3-5 shows that the spine is naturally curved. Figure 3-6 shows the curves more clearly. The two most evident curves are in the neck and lower back. These curves absorb the shock of normal movement and protect the upper body from jarring. Do not try to eliminate or exaggerate the natural curves. The dangers of doing so range from postural deviation to serious nerve and organ damage.

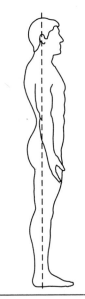

FIGURE 3-5 Line of gravity in correctly aligned body, side view

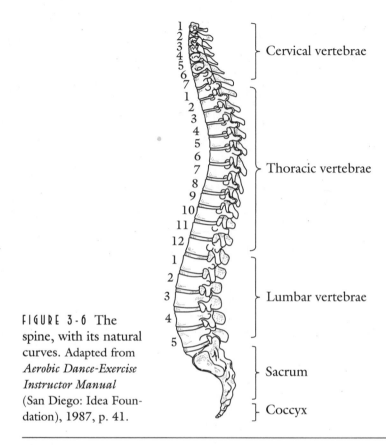

1
2
3
4
5
6
7
} Cervical vertebrae

1
2
3
4
5
6
7
8
9
10
11
12
} Thoracic vertebrae

1
2
3
4
5
} Lumbar vertebrae

} Sacrum

} Coccyx

FIGURE 3-6 The spine, with its natural curves. Adapted from *Aerobic Dance-Exercise Instructor Manual* (San Diego: Idea Foundation), 1987, p. 41.

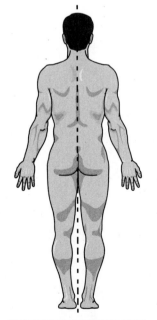

FIGURE 3-7 Line of gravity in correctly aligned body, back view

Figure 3-7 shows a correctly aligned body from the back. The line of gravity passes through these alignment reference points:

- The center of the head
- The midpoint of all vertebrae
- The cleft of the buttocks
- Midway between the heels

Now consider the correctly aligned body in detail, from head to toe.

Head and Neck

The head, the heaviest body segment, rests on the neck, which is a small flexible segment. The head should be carried directly atop the neck, not ahead or behind it. There should be a sense of the neck stretching away from the spine so that both the back and the front of the neck are long. With the head and neck in correct alignment, a vertical line can be drawn from the top of the ear to the middle of the shoulder girdle.

Shoulder Girdle

The shoulder girdle — consisting of the clavicle in front and the scapula in back — should be directly above the rib cage. The shoulder girdle is attached to the trunk only at the sternum (breastbone), allowing it to move freely. The shoulders should not be pulled back or allowed to slump forward; they should point directly to the side so that the chest is not collapsed and the shoulder blades are not pinched. The arms should hang freely in the sockets. The shoulders should be low enough and the neck "long" enough to maximize the distance between the shoulders and the ears.

Rib Cage

The rib cage floats above the pelvis and is connected in back to the spinal column. The rib cage should be pulled in toward the spine and lifted upward from the pelvis to create a long-waisted appearance.

Pelvis

The pelvis is the keystone of the skeleton. The tilt of the pelvis affects the posture of the entire body and the distribution of body weight over the feet. When the pelvis is in the correct, or neutral, alignment, it rests over the hip joints; it is not angled forward or backward. The natural curve in the lower spine is visible. When beginning dancers assume correct pelvic alignment, they usually sense a lengthening of the lumbar spine and a shortening of the abdominal muscles. Extreme forward or backward tilting of the pelvis can injure the lumbar spine and the muscles of the lower back.

Knees

The knee position, which is affected by the placement of the pelvis, should be directly above and in line with the direction of the toes. In the standing position, the knees should be slightly relaxed. Hyperextension (a locking or pressing too far back) of the knees is a common error.

Feet

Although the pelvis is the keystone of the skeletal structure, the feet provide the main base of support. In a static position, the greatest support is

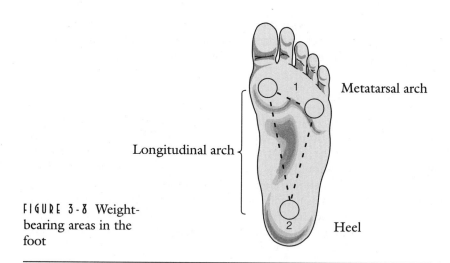

Metatarsal arch

Longitudinal arch

Heel

FIGURE 3-8 Weight-bearing areas in the foot

achieved when the weight of the body is equally distributed over the metatarsal arch (the ball of the foot), the base of the big toe, the base of the small toe, and the heel (see Figure 3-8). All the toes should remain in contact with the floor to provide the widest possible base of support. In addition, the longitudinal arch should be well lifted to prevent the ankle from rolling inward.

POSTURAL DEVIATIONS

When the body does not maintain correct alignment, postural deviations will occur. Because posture and the body's alignment are habitual, most people are not aware of their postural deviations. When a person has maintained a misaligned spine for 20 years and someone attempts to help him or her find correct alignment, the new position will feel odd and uncomfortable. It takes both muscle reconditioning and kinesthetic awareness of the correct placement in order to make a change in a person's posture and alignment. By giving appropriate kinesthetic cues, practicing the correct body position, and performing specific exercises to stretch and strengthen the misused muscles on a regular basis, an individual can improve alignment and posture.

The three primary postural deviations, lordosis, kyphosis, and scoliosis (see Figure 3-9), all are concerned with the alignment of the spinal column. All three can be temporary or permanent. They may be caused by fatigue or by a muscle, tendon, or ligament imbalance, which exercise

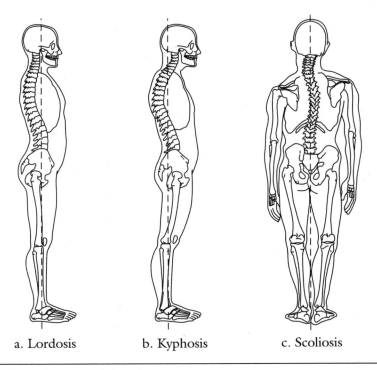

a. Lordosis   b. Kyphosis   c. Scoliosis

FIGURE 3-9 Postural deviations

and awareness can improve. If the deviations are caused by structural abnormalities of the bones, then exercise will not improve the condition. A
physician should be consulted. In correct alignment, there is a natural or
"neutral" curve in the spinal column (see Figure 3-6). This curve mini-
mizes excess stress on the spine and its surrounding soft tissues. In a deviation, the neutral curve becomes excessive.

Lordosis is an excessive curve of the lower or lumbar spine. In this
position, the pelvis has an increased anterior tilt, which increases the normal inward curve of the lower back. This spinal deviation is often accompanied by a protruding abdomen and buttocks, rounded shoulders,
and a forward head. Poor postural habits or jobs that require standing all
day can cause this excessive curve. For these situations, exercise and
awareness can help greatly to improve the alignment.

Kyphosis is an increase in the normal outward curve of the thoracic
vertebrae. This increased curve is often accompanied by round shoulders,
a sunken chest, and a forward head. Poor habits are the main reason for
this deviation. Sitting at a desk for many hours can exaggerate this posture. Exercise can help to improve the problem.

Scoliosis is a lateral curve of the spine. Unlike the other two deviations, it cannot be seen from the profile. In scoliosis, the vertebrae may rotate, causing a backward shift of the rib cage to one side. The pelvis as well as the shoulders may appear uneven. Often this deviation is structural. If this is the case, a physician should be seen for guidance.

If you were to analyze carefully how you stand, sit, carry and lift objects, and even sleep, you would understand how poor postural habits develop. By performing activities with a minimum of strain on our joints and muscles, we can improve our alignment and minimize our risk for lower back pain. To see changes in posture, three things must take place:

1. Kinesthetic awareness of the correct alignment
2. Muscle reconditioning of the imbalanced muscles
3. Performance of daily tasks with correct form

ALIGNMENT EXERCISES

The exercises described below will help you become kinesthetically aware of correct alignment. This means that you will be able to feel the correct alignment without having to look in a mirror. This is the first task to accomplish in order to improve posture. These exercises may be performed in 10 minutes and can serve as a pre–warm-up to dance class. It is recommended that they be performed daily until correct alignment becomes a habit.

Starting Position for Alignment Exercises   Lie on your back with your knees bent, the soles of your feet flat on the ground, your arms by the side of your body, and the palms of both hands flat on the floor (Figure 3-10). In this position, with the knees bent, the natural curve of the lower back is diminished somewhat to protect it from strain.

FIGURE 3-10 Starting position for alignment exercises

FIGURE 3-11 Aligning the shoulder girdle and expanding the back and chest

Exercise 1: Alignment of the Neck and Pelvis Assume the starting position and take deep breaths. As you exhale, allow your abdomen to contract. At the same time, attempt to lengthen your neck along the floor, pressing your chin slightly down. Hold this position, concentrating on the position of your neck, lower back, and abdomen. Repeat the exercise four times. Maintain the position of your abdomen, lower back, and neck throughout the remaining exercises.

Exercise 2: Alignment of the Shoulder Girdle Assume the starting position and place both hands on your hipbones. Keeping your elbows in contact with the floor, try to stretch to point your elbows toward the sides of the room (Figure 3-11). Hold for 10 seconds, then relax. Repeat this stretch four times. Although the movement of this exercise is slight, when executed properly it will expand the back and the chest equally. Maintain this back and chest expansion throughout the remaining exercises.

Exercise 3: Alignment of the Shoulder Girdle Assume the starting position, with your hands placed on your hipbones. Isolate your shoulders by lifting them forward off the floor (Figure 3-12). Hold this posi-

FIGURE 3-12 Aligning the shoulder girdle and maintaining neck alignment

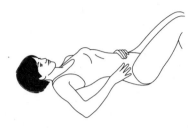

FIGURE 3-13 Aligning the rib cage

tion for 5 seconds. Relax and place your shoulders in contact with the floor. As this exercise is performed, attempt to create the greatest distance possible between your shoulders and your ears. This will help to maintain the correct shoulder and neck alignment. Repeat the exercise four times.

Exercise 4: Alignment of the Rib Cage Assume the starting position, with your hands on your hipbones. Lift your rib cage off the floor to create an extreme arch in your back, keeping your shoulders planted firmly on the floor (Figure 3-13). Reverse the action, pressing your rib cage back against the floor, or farther toward your spine. This position, with the rib cage pressed down, is correct alignment. Repeat the exercise four times, ending with your rib cage in its correct position against the floor.

Exercise 5: Placement of the Pelvis Assume the starting position, with your arms stretched to the side. Push your lower back against the floor. Relax and release your back to allow the natural curve of your spine. Repeat the exercise four times.

    After completing exercise 5, mentally review the correct alignment of the body parts:

- Abdominal muscles contracted
- Back and chest equally expanded, with elbows pointing to the side
- Neck and ears stretching away from the spine and shoulders
- Shoulders resting flat against the floor
- Legs straight, without the knees being locked
- Breathing full and easy

Come to a standing position.

Exercise 6: Alignment in a Standing Position Stand against a wall with your heels about 2 inches from the wall and your knees slightly bent.

TABLE 3-1 EXERCISES TO AVOID

To protect your alignment and to have the safest and most effective warm-up during the jazz dance class, it is suggested that these specific exercises be avoided. We have listed the regions of the body that are most prone to misalignment and injury.

REGION	EXERCISE	MODIFICATION
Lumbar and thoracic spine	Full sit-ups	Substitute curl-ups
	Toe touches	Substitute sustained supported stretch on floor
	Double leg raises	Substitute curl-ups
	Flat back bounces	Delete
	Unsupported lateral flexion	Place hand on thigh to support back
Cervical spine	Head drop to ceiling	Delete
	Yoga plough	Substitute gentle stretching, using hand to pull head forward
	Fast head circles	Perform slowly or delete
Knee	Lotus position	Substitute butterfly stretch with soles of feet together
	Hurdler's stretch	Change knee position of bent knee to touch inside of opposite leg

Assume the same body alignment you just experienced on the floor, keeping in mind the mental cues just outlined. Hold this position for a minimum of 20 seconds. Once you feel comfortable in this position, try to maintain this alignment while walking around the room.

Note the ballet positions used in this jazz dance, "Aretha," choreographed by Joseph Holmes and Randy Duncan.

CHAPTER 4

*B*ALLET FOR THE JAZZ DANCER

Classical ballet training develops line and form (the two- and three-dimensional images created by the dancer's body), muscle strength, joint flexibility, balance, and coordination. Ballet training is valuable to the jazz dancer because it provides a basic understanding of dance principles and instills the proper execution of dance techniques.

Ballet's principles and techniques developed in the seventeenth century and were founded on classical ideals of grace and beauty. The line and form of Greek statues provided an inspiration for early choreographers, who developed a technique based on their study and understanding of the body. Through the years the classical ideals of ballet have been maintained, but technical discoveries have aided the advancement of its technique.

This chapter outlines the ballet techniques, positions, movements, and vocabulary that are typically included in the jazz dance class. Because ballet developed primarily in France, the terms used are in French; since they describe the movements literally, English translations are included to help the student understand the essence of the particular movement. Dance combinations are built from these basic positions and movements. To follow the teacher's instructions, the student must be familiar with the basic vocabulary.

*T*URNOUT

Turnout is the outward rotation of the legs from the hip sockets. The turned-out position maximizes the dancer's balance because it provides a wider base of support than does a parallel position (Figure 4-1). Turnout also reveals more of the dancer's leg, gives a slimmer side view of the dancer, and facilitates sideward movement.

The degree of turnout is defined by the skeletal structure of the pelvic girdle and by the muscles controlling the rotation of the leg at the hip socket. To determine your natural turnout, stand with your feet in the parallel first position shown in Figure 4-1. Without moving your feet, rotate your legs outward from your hip joints. The end position is your

FIGURE 4-1 Ballet
positions of the feet

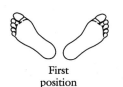

First
position

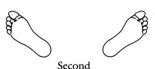

Second
position

Third
position

Fourth
position

Fifth
position

natural turnout. A common error is to turn the feet out farther than the legs are actually turned out at the hip joints—a practice that can result in injury to the muscles and ligaments of the hip, knee, and ankle joints. The range of turnout can be increased with flexibility exercises for the muscles surrounding the hip joint and strength-building exercises for the muscles that rotate the legs outward.

BALLET FOOT POSITIONS

In ballet, all movements proceed from, and end in, the five basic positions of the feet, which are executed in turnout.

BALLET ARM POSITIONS

Although positions of the feet are standard in all schools, or methods, of ballet, the positions of the arms are not. Of the three schools of ballet—Cecchetti, French, and Russian—each has individual arm positions and variations. Consult a ballet dictionary for detailed descriptions of these methods. The arm descriptions and definitions used in this text are based on the Cecchetti method.

In all positions, a specific manner of holding the arms is used to create the graceful ballet line: The arms are held slightly rounded and slightly forward of the body, with the shoulders down and relaxed; the wrist and hand are held as an extension of the arm, with the thumb held inward toward the palm and the fingers relaxed.

First Position

As Figure 4-2 shows, in first position the arms are held slightly rounded at the side.

Second Position

As Figure 4-3 shows, in second position the arms are held horizontally and slightly rounded.

Third Position

Figure 4-4 shows third position: One arm is held slightly rounded to the side and midway between first and second positions. The other arm is held in fifth position low.

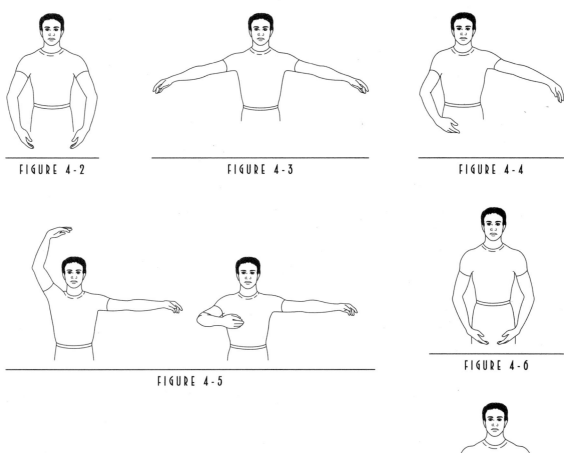

FIGURE 4-2   FIGURE 4-3   FIGURE 4-4

FIGURE 4-5

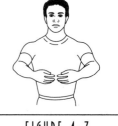

FIGURE 4-6

Fourth Position

Figure 4-5 shows fourth position: One arm is held in second position. The other arm may be held in either fifth position front or fifth position high.

FIGURE 4-7

Fifth Position

There are three fifth positions:

Fifth Position en bas The arms are held slightly rounded in front of the thighs, as in Figure 4-6.

Fifth Position en avant The arms are held slightly rounded in front of the chest, parallel to the floor. Figure 4-7 shows fifth position front.

Fifth Position en haut The arms are held slightly rounded over the head, as in Figure 4-8.

FIGURE 4-8

BALLET MOVEMENTS

All ballet movements are performed in the turned-out position. To maintain turnout during leg movements, certain rules should be followed:

- When the leg is extended to the front, the heel leads the movement and continually presses forward to maintain the turned-out position of the leg.
- When the leg is extended to the side, the heel presses forward as the leg extends on the diagonal line of the turnout.
- When the leg is extended to the rear, the big toe leads the movement, while the heel presses forward, maintaining the turned-out position of the leg. The pelvis should face front squarely.

In jazz dance, the ballet movements described in the section that follows are also performed in the parallel positions (see Figure 5-1).

Pliés

There are two principal *pliés,* the *demi-plié* and the *grand plié.* The *demi-plié* is a half-bending of the knees without lifting the heels from the floor (Figure 4-9). The *grand plié* is a full bending of the knees, passing through the *demi-plié* and lowering until only the balls of the feet remain on the floor (Figure 4-10). A *grand plié* in second position is an exception. In it the heels never leave the floor. In straightening the legs from the *grand plié,* it is essential to pass through the *demi-plié,* returning the heels to the floor before regaining the full vertical position. In all *pliés,*

Correct   Incorrect

FIGURE 4-9 The *demi-plié*

| Correct | Incorrect | Second position |

FIGURE 4-10   The *grand plié*

the movement should be continuous. Because *pliés* require balance and strength, beginning students are encouraged to practice them at the barre.

PRECAUTIONS

- In all *plié* movements keep the pressure off your knees by maintaining good body alignment.
- In all *plié* movements keep your knees directly in line with your feet and toes.

MOVEMENT TIPS

- Do not execute the *grand plié* until you have mastered the *demi-plié*.
- In the *grand plié*, the *demi-plié* must be completed before the heels are allowed to rise off the floor.

The *Relevé*

The *relevé* ("rise") is a rise onto the balls of the feet, with the legs straight and the torso held erect (Figure 4-11). The weight of the body must be

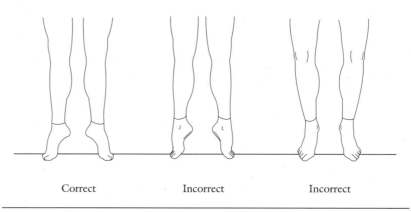

Correct	Incorrect	Incorrect

FIGURE 4-11 The *relevé*

centered between the first and second toes to maintain correct alignment of the ankle. The toes should be extended and spread open against the floor for balance. The upper body is lifted as the balls of the feet press into the floor on the rise, and it remains lifted as the heels are lowered to the floor on the descent. When the *relevé* is performed, the movement should be smooth and continuous as it is in the *plié*.

PRECAUTIONS

- In all *relevé* movements keep the pressure off your knee and ankle joints by maintaining correct body alignment.
- Avoid stressing ligaments of your ankle by keeping the weight centered over your first and second toes.

Battements

A *battement* ("beating") is an extension of the leg that brushes the foot along the floor. *Battements* can be performed to the front, side, or back. When battements are performed to the front, side, back, and again to the side, the term *en croix* is used to describe this action. The level of the leg and the quality of the movement define the type of *battement*.

The *Battement Tendu* The *battement tendu* ("stretched beating") is a brush of the straight leg to its full extension, with only the toes remaining on the floor (Figure 4-12). The foot must release contact with the floor in a sequential movement from the heel through the ball of the foot to the toes. The closing of the *tendu* reverses the sequential movement.

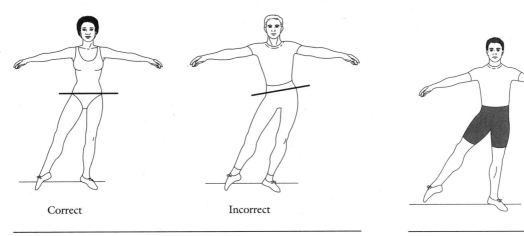

Correct   Incorrect

FIGURE 4-12 The *battement tendu*

FIGURE 4-13 The *battement dégagé*

FIGURE 4-14 The *grand battement*

The *Battement Dégagé* The *battement dégagé* ("released beating") is a quick brush of the straight leg through *tendu* to a position slightly off the floor (Figure 4-13). The rapidity of this movement trains the foot to work quickly; it is therefore essential that the foot is not lifted higher than 4 inches off the floor.

The *Grand Battement* The *grand battement* ("large beating") is a high, straight-leg lift, passing through the *tendu* and *dégagé* and carrying the leg quickly to 90 degrees or higher (Figure 4-14). The return of the *grand battement* passes through the closing movement of the *tendu*. Lifting the leg quickly and lowering it slowly is an essential technique in *grand battement*.

MOVEMENT TIPS

- In all *battement* movements do not shift your weight too far over the supporting leg. Keeping your weight as centered as possible avoids unnecessary stress on the ligaments supporting your pelvis and lower back.
- When performing the *battement tendu,* do not bear weight on the extended foot.
- When you perform *grand battements,* the action should be a sweeping motion so that the hamstring muscles on the back of your leg can be the main muscle group that will lift your leg.

The *Rond De Jambe*

The *rond de jambe* ("circling of the leg") (Figure 4-15) is a movement in which the working leg traces a semicircle on the ground (*a terre*) or in the air (*a l'air*). When the leg travels in an arc from the front to the back, it is called *en dehors* ("outward"). When the action goes from the back to the front, it is called *en dedans* ("inward"). When a *rond de jambe* is performed, it is important to stabilize the torso and the hip. The purpose of the exercise is to create flexibility and mobility in the hip joint socket and to improve turnout in the hip joint.

MOVEMENT TIPS

- Keep your body weight centered over the standing leg with correct hip alignment.
- Do not allow your hips to move at all; let your leg create the arc.
- When your foot passes through the first position, as it completes the arc, maintain the turn-out of your leg and foot.

Ballet Combinations Used in Jazz Dance Class

COMBINATION 1

Counts

2 down, 2 up   *Demi-plié*

Repeat

FIGURE 4-15 *Rond de jambe*

4 down, 4 up   *Grand plié*

2 up, 4 balance, 2 down   *Relevé*

Perform this combination in first, second, fourth, and fifth positions.
Repeat in parallel first and second positions.

COMBINATION 2

Counts

4   *Battement tendu* (front two times)

4   *Battement tendu* (side two times)

4   *Battement tendu* (back two times)

4   *Battement tendu* (side two times)

Repeat in parallel position.

COMBINATION 3

Counts

    4   *Battement dégagé* (front two times)

    4   *Battement dégagé* (side two times)

    4   *Battement dégagé* (back two times)

    4   *Battement dégagé* (side two times)

Perform in turn-out and parallel positions.

COMBINATION 4

Counts

    8   *Grand battement* (front two times)

    8   *Grand battement* (side two times)

    8   *Grand battement* (back two times)

    8   *Grand battement* (side two times)

Perform only in turn-out position.

COMBINATION 5

Counts

    8   *Rond de jambe en dehors*

Repeat four times, making sure to close in first position at the completion of each one.

    8   *Rond de jambe en dedans*

Repeat four times, making sure to close in first position at the completion of each one.

Repeat all with the supporting leg in *plié.*

BALLET POSITIONS USED IN JAZZ DANCE

The *Arabesque*

FIGURE 4-16 The *arabesque*

The *arabesque* takes its name from a form of Moorish ornament. In this position, the body is supported on one leg, which may be straight or in *demi-plié,* while the other leg is fully extended to the rear and raised as high as possible to the back (Figure 4-16). The arms are held in various harmonious positions, usually with one arm extended forward to create a long straight line from the fingertips of the extended front arm to the toes of the extended leg. The hips and shoulders should remain square to the direction the body is facing. The upper torso should be held upright, although as the extended leg is raised to greater heights, the body may lean slightly forward to maintain the long straight line.

FIGURE 4-17
Examples of the
attitude

PRECAUTION

- Keep your back straight and your torso upright. Arching the upper or lower back causes unnecessary pressure on the back.

The *Attitude*

The *attitude* ("pose") is thought to be derived from the statue of Mercury by Giovanni da Bologna. The dancer balances on one leg, with the opposite leg extended, knee bent, to the front, side, or rear (Figure 4-17). The thigh of the bent leg is parallel to the floor, and the toe is as high as, or slightly below, the height of the knee.

The *Coupé*

The *coupé* (Figure 4-18) ("to cut") is a position and a small intermediary step that is usually done as a preparation or impetus for another step. The ankle of one leg is positioned at the ankle of the supporting leg either in front or in back. The *coupé* occurs when the lifted foot "cuts" away and takes the place of the supporting leg.

The *Passé*

In the *passé* ("passed through"), the dancer balances on one leg, with the opposite leg bent and the toe pointed to touch the hollow of the knee of the standing leg (Figure 4-19). When the *passé* is performed in turnout, the standing leg and the bent knee are turned out as far as possible. In jazz dance, the *passé* is also executed in the parallel position, with the knees of

FIGURE 4-18 The *coupé*

both legs pointing straight ahead and the foot of the bent leg pressed firmly against the knee of the standing leg.

Passé turn-out

BASIC DANCE PRINCIPLES

In both ballet and jazz dance, certain principles of movement must be applied at all times. These principles relate to weight placement, the pointing of the feet, jumps, and turns. The dance student should continually work on embodying these principles until their execution becomes automatic.

Shifting the Weight

When the body shifts support from both feet to one foot, or from one foot to the other, a shift of weight must also occur. If balance is to be maintained, the shift of weight must occur without a change of the pelvis, which should remain horizontal throughout the movement (Figure 4-20). Pulling up on the abdominal muscles will keep the pelvis in its correct position and the weight lifted out of the legs, thus enabling a smooth shift of weight.

Pointing the Foot

Always in ballet, and most often in jazz dance, the foot must point. If it is not pointed it is flexed, but it is never dangling. When pointing (which is also called extension of the ankle), certain guidelines are helpful:

Passé parallel

FIGURE 4-19 The *passé*

- Think of a straight line from the top of the knee to the ankle and finally to the big toe.
- Keep the toes long and extended. Do not let them curl under.
- Create the greatest arch of the foot by using the instep and muscles of the longitudinal arch.
- The foot is said to be sickled if it leans toward the big toe or the little toe. Do not sickle the foot inward or outward. Maintain the straight line that extends from the knee to the ankle and through the big toe.
- Practice pointing the foot and also performing the opposite movement, flexion. When flexing the foot, pull the whole foot back toward the knee and—as with pointing—keep the toes, ankle, and knee in one straight line.

Jumps

The ability to jump high and land softly and smoothly demands the application of important ballet principles. These principles not only help to

Correct   Incorrect

FIGURE 4-20 Weight shifts must occur without a shift in the pelvis.

achieve a beautiful and exciting jump, but are also necessary to prevent injury to the dancer's knees, ankles, and feet.

Four principles must be applied when performing jumps of any kind:

1. The dancer must begin all jumps from the *demi-plié* position.
2. To attain the height of the jump, the dancer must press off the floor by fully extending (pointing) the feet.
3. The dancer must land from the jump on the balls of the feet, rolling through to the heels.
4. All jumps must end with a return to the *demi-plié* position.

Turns

Spectators are always entranced with the dancer's ability to turn, and beginning dancers are always amazed at how dizzy they become when first attempting to turn. The secret to alleviating the dizziness and acquiring the ability to do multiple turns is spotting. **Spotting** is the ability of the dancer to keep the eyes focused on one spot as long as possible while turning the body. When eye contact on the focus spot can no longer be maintained, the dancer quickly turns the head, immediately regaining focus on the chosen spot, which should be at, or slightly above, eye level. It is best to start the practice of spotting by executing a walking turn slowly in place, gradually increasing the speed until the whip of the head is quick and smooth and the eyes focus quickly. When spotting, keep the eye focus level and attempt to keep your chin parallel to the floor.

Other ballet movements are often used in jazz dance. These movements and their jazz names are included in Chapters 6, 7, and 8.

Liz Williamson

CHAPTER 5

*B*ASIC JAZZ POSITIONS

First position

Second position

No third
parallel

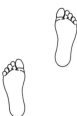

Fourth position

Fifth position

FIGURE 5-1 Foot
positions

Ballet developed in the academic environment in which vocabulary was defined by classic ideals and enlarged as technical knowledge of flexibility and strength grew. Jazz dance, in contrast, was developed through improvisation and through the personalities and styles of its performers. Developing as it did, jazz dance had no clear-cut vocabulary for many years. In spite of this problem, and even though each school of jazz dance has its own unique set of movements as created by an instructor, certain positions and steps have become a universally accepted part of jazz dance. This chapter describes the basic positions generally used in a jazz dance class.

*J*AZZ FOOT POSITIONS

In jazz dance, the positions of the feet include the turned-out ballet positions illustrated in Chapter 4, as well as the same positions with the feet in parallel. The parallel counterparts are illustrated in Figure 5-1.

*J*AZZ ARM POSITIONS

In addition to the ballet arms described in Chapter 4, a variety of arm positions are distinctive to jazz dance. The arm is often straight, with the fingers spread wide open. This hand position is referred to as the **jazz hand** (Figure 5-2). The **jazz arm** also can be inverted so that the elbows are facing down and the wrist can be extended or flexed (Figure 5-3). Another position commonly used in jazz dance is **jazz fifth** or the jazz V position. Here the arms are lifted to the diagonal with the palms facing either down or up but with the elbows fully extended (Figure 5-4).

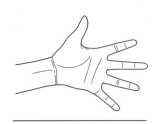

FIGURE 5-2 The jazz
hand

61

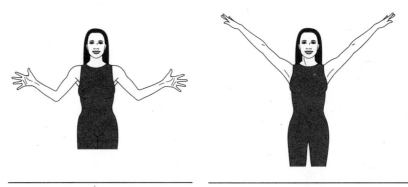

FIGURE 5-3 The jazz arm   FIGURE 5-4 Jazz fifth position

Basic Body Positions

Certain positions are used continually throughout a jazz dance class. These positions are used during the warm-up as well as in combinations to create a variety of locomotor movements. It is important when first learning these positions to execute them precisely so that their accurate execution will become habit. Included are precautionary statements that encourage safe positioning. Do not hesitate to use a mirror to check your position.

The number of repetitions that you can perform will be determined by your instructor and your level of strength and experience. Never continue an exercise if you are too tired to maintain the correct position. Working incorrectly can lead to serious injury and misalignment.

The Arch

The arch position of the spine is a curve of the torso upward and backward, and is merely an arch of the cervical and thoracic spine (Figure 5-5). The hips do not change position. In the arch position contract the buttocks and abdominal muscles so that there is limited use of the lower back. There should be a feeling of lifting through the neck as opposed to a dropping of the head.

PRECAUTIONS

- Do not drop your head completely. This causes unnecessary pressure on your spine.
- Tighten the gluteals so that there is no stress on your lower back.

Correct   Incorrect

FIGURE 5-5 The arch

Correct

The Contraction

The term *contraction* indicates a drawing in, or shortening, of body parts. Although the term may refer to any body part, in jazz, contraction often refers to the torso. In a torso contraction, the front of the torso is concave so that the spine curves outward slightly (Figure 5-6). The lower back is rounded, the abdomen is hollowed, and the pelvis is pulled forward with the shoulders held directly above the hips. The chest and shoulders should not slump, and the knees should be slightly bent.

Incorrect

FIGURE 5-6 The contraction

PRECAUTIONS

- Body height should not decrease significantly; only a rounding of the torso should occur.
- Make sure abdominal and buttocks muscles are tight.

The Flat Back

The flat back is a position in which the dancer bends forward from the hips at a 90-degree angle (Figure 5-7). The back is straight and parallel to the floor. Flat back is also referred to as tabletop position. In the flat-back position, the body weight should be over the toes with the heels just slightly in contact with the floor. The entire spine, from the base of the skull to the tailbone, should be in one flat line parallel to the floor.

FIGURE 5-7 The flat back

PRECAUTIONS

- Because of the possible strain on your lower back, your knees should not be locked when in this position.
- Tightly contract the abdominal muscles to avoid unnecessary pressure on your lower back.
- Your neck should be in line with your spine; do not lift your head.

FIGURE 5-8 The diagonal flat back

The Diagonal Flat Back

In the diagonal flat-back position, the dancer bends from the hips until the straight back is parallel to the floor and then shifts the torso sideways until it is diagonal to the direction in which the legs are facing (Figure 5-8). The dancer must stretch equally on both sides.

PRECAUTIONS

- Maintain an equal stretch on both sides of your body.
- To avoid abnormal twisting of your lower back and spine, do not allow your hips to shift from the center alignment.
- Tightly contract the abdominal muscles to avoid unnecessary pressure on your lower back.
- Your neck should be in line with your spine; do not lift your head.

The Hinge

The hinge is a tilt of the torso with an imaginary oblique straight line that passes from the tip of the ear through the shoulder, hip, and knee (Figure 5-9). Usually, the dancer performs the hinge in a standing position with knees bent and heels off the floor. The beginning dancer should execute this position on the knees before attempting the standing version.

Correct

Correct

Incorrect

FIGURE 5-9 The hinge

> ### PRECAUTIONS
>
> - Tightly contract the abdominal muscles to avoid unnecessary pressure on your lower back.
> - Maintain a straight diagonal body line, keeping your head in line with your shoulder, hips, and knees.

The Lateral

The lateral position is any bend to the side. The bend can initiate from the waist (Figure 5-10) or can be merely a tilt of the head and shoulders to the side.

Incorrect   Correct

FIGURE 5-10 The lateral

PRECAUTIONS

- Your body should not lean forward or backward when executing this position; your body must bend directly to the side.
- As in any position, the abdominal muscles must be tightly contracted to avoid unnecessary pressure on your lower back.

The Lunge

The lunge is a position in which one foot is advanced as far as possible with the knee bent while the other foot remains stationary with the leg straight (Figure 5-11). The legs are either parallel or turned out in second or fourth position. Torso position can vary.

PRECAUTIONS

- Make sure your weight is always over the bent knee.
- Keep your heels in contact with the floor.
- Keep your knees in line with your toes.
- Keep the bent knee in line with your ankle joint.

FIGURE 5-11 The lunge

The Jazz Sit

The jazz sit is a position in which the body weight is maintained on one leg (straight). The knee of the opposite leg is bent, with the foot in a forced arch position (Figure 5-12).

PRECAUTION

- Do not roll onto your big toe, but keep your weight over all five toes.

FIGURE 5-12 The jazz sit

The Jazz Split

A jazz split is a half-split position on the floor, in which the front leg is straight and the rear leg is bent as in *attitude* (Figure 5-13). The jazz split is often reached from a standing position. See Chapter 7 for a complete description of the jazz split.

PRECAUTIONS

- Your weight should be over your front leg when starting from a standing position.
- Your weight is on the outside of your foot so that turnout is maintained.

FIGURE 5-13 The jazz split

Gus Giordano jazz dance, Chicago 1989: "Gang Hep"

CHAPTER 6
*T*HE JAZZ DANCE WARM-UP

A warm-up is like tuning a fine instrument. The body, the jazz dancer's instrument, must be tuned to respond to the demands placed on it during a jazz dance class. Often a class warm-up begins with fairly vigorous exercises. Because of this vigorous warm-up, the dancer should allow approximately 10 minutes before class for an individual pre–warm-up. The pre–warm-up increases body temperature through light to moderate exercise. During this time, extra attention should be paid to warming up any area of the body that is weak or prone to injury.

*P*ROPER STRETCHING TECHNIQUES

Careless execution of movements and stretches can result in muscle tears and damage. Adhering to the proper stretching techniques described below will provide the safest and most effective warm-up. (See also Table 6-1 for a sample warm-up routine.)

- A long, sustained (static) stretch rather than a bouncing (ballistic) stretch is best for achieving flexibility. Muscles have a stretch reflex; when you bounce, the reflex causes the muscles to react by tightening rather than by stretching.
- When you want to increase flexibility, it is necessary to stretch to the point of mild tension and then relax in that position for 15–30 seconds. Then release the position and repeat the stretch.
- When stretching a muscle, contract the opposing muscle. For example, contract the front of your thigh (quadriceps) and then follow this with a passive stretch for the back of your thigh (hamstrings).
- Perform all of the movements with correct alignment. Avoid postural misalignment of your lower back and knees.
- Relax during flexibility stretching.

TABLE 6-1 WARM-UP ROUTINE

EXERCISE	REPETITIONS	COUNTS
Lunge with opposition stretch	4	2 each
Plié in second	1	8
Parallel second-position forward straight/bent legs	1	4 each
Roll up to start position	1	8
Repeat all three more times		
Side stretch	4 right, 4 left	1 each
Back stretch	4	1 each
Flat-back position	4	1 each
Parallel second-position forward bent/stretch legs	1	4 each
Roll up to start position	1	8
Repeat from side stretch three more times		
Body wave	4	4 each
Repeat body wave	4	2 each
Parallel first-position forward stretch; end with legs straight	4	8
Hand walk	1	16
Modified push-ups	8-16	4 each
Runner's lunge	8 in each position	1 each
Come to parallel first with hands on floor and roll up to vertical		16

The counts and repetitions may be varied. After the sample warm-up routine is executed, the other aspects of the warm-up should be performed. The order of the exercises to follow this routine will vary depending on the instructor.

- A series of *pliés* and *battements* as outlined in Chapter 4
- Floor stretches
- Isolations, balancing exercises, preparation for jumps and/or a series of jumps

- Avoid holding your breath during any phase of the stretch; not breathing indicates a lack of relaxation. If your body vibrates or shakes during any of the stretches, ease up—you cannot relax if you are straining.

As you progress through the stretches, keep in mind that flexibility is highly individual. Not all of the exercises are appropriate for all people. Flexibility varies widely among people and among the joints and muscles within each individual. Anatomical abnormalities and improper exercise techniques can result in injury. If you perform an exercise correctly but experience abnormal pain, discontinue that particular exercise and seek professional advice regarding the problem.

The following section describes stretches that can be performed before class and then follows with typical stretches used for the jazz dance warm-up. Remember, some of these exercises are used for warming up the body, so pulsating into the movement is acceptable. When working to increase flexibility, follow the stretching techniques previously outlined.

Floor Exercises for the Ankle, Knee, and Hip Joints

The pre–warm-up may begin in any position. However, it is good to begin by lying on the floor to relieve the body of the additional stress of working against the pull of gravity, so that full attention can be paid to maintaining proper body position. The following simple exercises may be used in warming up the ankle, knee, and hip joints.

Exercise 1: Toe Flex   Lying flat on your back, flex and point your foot, moving only your toes and metatarsal arch (Figure 6-1) (do not move your ankle joint). Repeat eight times with each foot.

Exercise 2: Ankle Flex   Lying flat on your back, flex and extend your foot at your ankle (Figure 6-2). Repeat eight times with each foot.

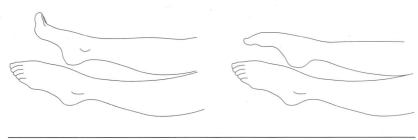

FIGURE 6-1   FIGURE 6-2

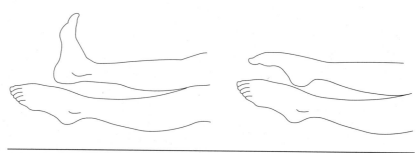

FIGURE 6-3

Exercise 3: Ankle Rotations Lying flat on your back, rotate your ankles in both directions (Figure 6-3). Repeat eight times with each foot.

Exercise 4: Knee to Chest Lying flat on your back with your knees bent and the soles of your feet flat on the floor, raise one knee toward your chest (Figure 6-4). Return to the starting position and repeat with the opposite knee. Repeat four times on each side.

Exercise 5: Lower-Back Twist Lying flat on your back, extend arms straight out to the sides, palms down on the floor. Lift one knee toward your chest. Twisting your lower back, lower your knee to the floor by the opposite arm (Figure 6-5). Relax in this position. Lift your knee back to your chest and lower your leg to the floor. Repeat four times on each side.

While still on the floor, perform the alignment exercises outlined in Chapter 3.

FIGURE 6-4

FIGURE 6-5

Standing Exercises for the Upper Torso and Weight-Bearing Joints

Once the student has completed a floor pre—warm-up, additional standing exercises can be used to warm up the upper torso and weight-bearing joints.

Exercise 1: Head Rolls   If you have no history of misalignment in your cervical spine, perform four head rolls to the right. Begin by lowering your right ear toward your right shoulder. Then roll your chin to your chest, bring your left ear to your left shoulder, and then raise your head back to correct alignment. Repeat rolling your head four times to the left. Do not drop your head to your back because this can create undue pressure on your cervical spine. Do not do this exercise if your neck is chronically fatigued.

Exercise 2: Arm Circles   Repeat four times forward, four times backward.

Exercise 3: Waist Bends   Bend side to side a total of eight times.

Exercise 4: Foot Roll and Prance   Stand with your feet in parallel first position. Bend one knee, rolling through the ball of your foot to the pointed foot. Finally, lift the tip of your toe a few inches above the floor. Return your foot to the floor, reversing the foot's action. Figure 6-6 shows this exercise. Repeat several times at a slow tempo. Do the exercise at a quicker tempo, springing your foot off the floor. Repeat with the opposite foot.

Exercise 5: *Attitude* Leg Swings   This exercise may be done using the barre for support. Stand with your feet turned out. Lift your knee to the side *attitude* position, then swing your leg across your body in front of the supporting leg. Reverse the swing, returning your leg to the side *attitude* position. Figure 6-7 shows this exercise. Repeat several swings on each leg. This exercise will help warm up the front and inner thigh muscles and the hip joints.

FIGURE 6-7

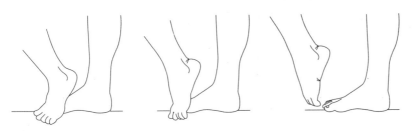

FIGURE 6-6

STANDING STRETCHES

These exercises are used mainly as a means to increase the temperature of the muscles, raise the body's intake of oxygen, and gradually increase the blood flow to the heart. The movements initially are performed at a slow pace, with a gradual increase in speed as the body gets warmer. By performing standing exercises before sitting exercises, the body is allowed to get a general warm-up before executing the more demanding floor stretches. The order of standing exercises and then floor exercises is not absolute, however; some teachers prefer the opposite order. In either case, to get maximum benefit from the warm-up period, take it easy when you first begin.

The Lunge with Opposition Stretch

The torso stretch can be performed in any of the foot positions. As the right arm reaches up toward the ceiling, the right knee bends (Figure 6-8). Body weight remains centered over both legs, causing the left hip to lift. The stretch is then performed on the opposite side of the body.

FIGURE 6-8 The lunge with opposition stretch

PRECAUTIONS

- Try not to overextend your rib cage; keep the line of your torso long and unbroken.
- Always keep your knees in line with your toes.
- Tightly contract the abdominal muscles to avoid unnecessary strain on your lower back.

The Parallel Second-Position Forward Stretch/Straight Knees

Standing in parallel second position, bend over to bring your hands as close to the floor as possible while keeping your knees straight (Figure 6-9). Perform this in combination with the next stretch.

FIGURE 6-9 The parallel second-position forward stretch with straight knees

The Parallel Second-Position Forward Stretch/Bent Knees

Standing in parallel second position, bend your knees and reach your hands through your legs as far as possible (Figure 6-10). Slowly straighten your legs while rolling your torso up to a vertical position.

FIGURE 6-10 The parallel second-position forward stretch with bent knees

Incorrect

PRECAUTIONS

- Do not lock your knees in the straight-leg stretch. Keep them slightly loose.
- Keep your weight over the balls of your feet at all times.
- Relax your neck so that the cervical spine is not pinched.

The Side Stretch

The side stretch, or lateral stretch, is usually performed in second position with turnout. With the arms extended vertically, reach as far to the side as possible by stretching the waist and rib cage while keeping the back straight (Figure 6-11). This can be performed in a *plié* position as well as with straight legs. The side stretch also can be performed with the arms in a variety of positions such as the lower arm rounding in front of the body or the lower arm resting on the thigh. People with lower back problems should place the arm on the thigh to help support the back.

Correct

FIGURE 6-11
The side stretch

PRECAUTIONS

- Do not bend forward; reach **directly** to the side.
- Do not overextend your rib cage; maintain proper alignment of your spine.
- Do not elevate your shoulder; stretch through your waist.

FIGURE 6-12 The parallel first-position forward stretch

The Parallel First-Position Forward Stretch

Standing in parallel first position and keeping your knees straight, bend over to place your hands on the floor. Keeping your hands on the floor, fully bend your knees, allowing your heels to release from the floor (Figure 6-12). Try to lift your heels as high off the floor as possible and stretch your feet in this position. Next, keeping your hands on the floor, return your heels to the floor and straighten your legs.

PRECAUTIONS

- Make sure to relax your neck in the straight-leg position.
- Do not lock your knees in the straight-leg stretch; keep them slightly loose.
- Keep your weight over the balls of your feet at all times.

The Body Wave

The body wave, or the body roll, is a sequential movement of the torso that is easily learned from a bent-knee flat back position. Start by contracting or rounding the lower back, and move the contraction sequentially up the spine, passing through a hinge position. The chin should rest on the chest until the "wave" reaches the neck. At that point, the chin will lift to the ceiling and the "wave" will complete in an arch position of the upper torso. Figure 6-13 shows the sequence of the movements. The body wave is usually a smooth movement and is performed to achieve spinal flexibility. The speed of the movement will determine its difficulty.

FIGURE 6-13 The body wave

Ultimately, the goal is to be able to execute the movement as quickly as possible.

PRECAUTIONS

- Tightly contract your abdominals to avoid unnecessary pressure to your lower back.
- Keep your chest and shoulders expanded.
- Begin the movement at your tailbone.

The Back Stretch

Perform the back stretch, or released stretch, in a parallel first or second position. Place your hands on your hipbones, with your elbows pressed forward. Slightly bend your knees, tighten your buttocks, arch your upper back, and lift your chin to the ceiling (Figure 6-14).

FIGURE 6-14
The back stretch

PRECAUTIONS

- Tightly contract your abdominal muscles to avoid unnecessary pressure to your lower back.
- Tighten your buttocks to press your hips forward for maximum stretch.
- Keep your chest and shoulders expanded.

FIGURE 6-15 The hand walk

The Hand Walk

From parallel first position with your hands on the floor, walk your hands
as far away from your feet as possible, keeping your heels in contact with
the floor (Figure 6-15). Try to keep your back flat during the hand walk.
Hold the stretch and then walk your hands back toward your feet. When
properly executed, this exercise stretches the hamstring muscles at the
back of the thigh and the Achilles tendon, which runs from the heel to
the back of the calf muscles.

PRECAUTIONS

- Tighten your abdominal muscles to avoid unnecessary pressure
  on your lower back.
- Keep your neck in line with your spine.
- Keep your knees relaxed.

The Runner's Lunge

This stretch is specifically for the Achilles tendon and the muscles of the
thigh and hip joint. From the parallel fourth-position lunge, place your
hands on the floor on either side of your forward bent knee. In this position, the heel of your front foot must remain on the floor. Your back leg
should be straight, foot fully flexed, with your toes pressed against the
floor. Keeping your hands on the floor, straighten your front leg while
pressing the heel of your back foot to the floor. Attempt to keep your
back flat, pressing your chest toward your front knee. For additional
stretch, flex the foot of your front leg, lifting your toes off the floor. Figure 6-16 shows the sequence of movements. Return to the lunge position and repeat the stretch sequence on the opposite leg.

FIGURE 6-16
The runner's lunge

ON-THE-FLOOR STRETCHES

The stretches presented on the floor should never be performed without prior warm-up. It is essential to get the body very warm to get the maximum benefit from these excellent stretches. To achieve maximum flexibility, follow the directions for stretching techniques that were outlined at the beginning of this chapter.

FIGURE 6-17 The parallel first-position stretch

The Parallel First-Position Stretch

This exercise stretches the hamstring muscles at the back of the thigh. In a straight-back sitting position, with your legs extended forward, keep your back flat and attempt to reach your ankles (Figure 6-17). Your feet may be pointed or flexed.

The Soles-of-the-Feet-Together Stretch

Sitting with the soles of your feet together and your knees bent, hold your ankles and stretch gently forward (Figure 6-18). Your back should be flat, pressing the pelvic girdle forward. In this position, a flexible dancer may use the pressure of the lower arm and elbow against the thighs to gently push the thighs toward the floor to increase the flexibility of the hip joints.

FIGURE 6-18 The soles-of-the-feet-together stretch

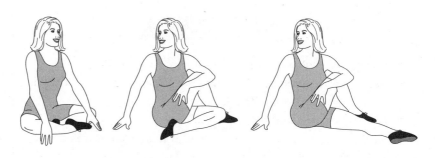

FIGURE 6-19 The pretzel

PRECAUTION

- For the soles-of-the-feet-together stretch (see page 79), do not put pressure on your knees at any time.

The Pretzel

Sitting with your back erect, cross your legs as shown in Figure 6-19. Lift your right leg and place your right foot on the outside of your left thigh, keeping all five toes in contact with the floor. Keep your back erect and pull your right knee toward your chest with your left arm while pressing your hip toward the floor. Perform the stretch with your left leg. This exercise also can be performed with the bottom leg straight.

PRECAUTIONS

- Do not round your shoulders; keep your chest "open" and your spine erect.
- Do not lift your hips off the floor.

Second-Position Straddle Stretches

Sitting with your back straight, open your legs as wide as possible to a straddle position (Figure 6-20). Your hips should remain on the floor, and your knees should face the ceiling during all straddle-stretch variations. All are excellent for increasing hip-joint and leg flexibility.

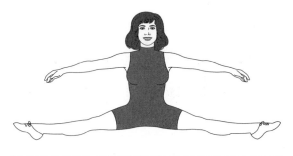

FIGURE 6-20 Second-position straddle stretch

FIGURE 6-21 The forward stretch

PRECAUTIONS

- In all straddle stretches make sure to keep your legs turned out from your hip joint.
- Keep both hips on the ground.
- Do not let your knees roll in. Direct them toward the ceiling.

The Forward Stretch   Holding your legs in turnout, press your chest forward toward the floor. This stretch may be done with your back rounded or flat and your feet pointed or flexed (Figure 6-21). As you stretch forward, place your hands on the floor in front of you to help support the weight of your torso and prevent strain to your lower back. In addition, take the precautions recommended for all straddle stretches.

The Side Stretch   Place your right arm down, palm up from your elbow on the floor, either inside or outside your right leg. Reach your left arm overhead while stretching from your waist toward your right leg. Hold your back straight, and place both hips solidly on the floor (Figure 6-22). Reverse the stretch.

FIGURE 6-22
The side stretch

FIGURE 6-23 The toward-the-leg stretch

The Toward-the-Leg Stretch   Twist from your waist as far as possible toward your right leg. Reach toward your right ankle with both hands, gently pulling your chest toward your right leg. Your left hip should remain in contact with the floor (Figure 6-23). This stretch may be done with your back rounded or flat and your feet pointed or flexed. Repeat the stretch toward your left leg. Take the precautions recommended for all straddle stretches.

The Knee-Bend Stretch

This exercise stretches the hamstrings. Perform this stretch while lying on the floor with your legs together and fully extended (Figure 6-24). Pull one knee to your chest, grasping your leg under your thigh. The leg remaining on the floor must remain straight and fully extended. From this position extend your bent leg to the ceiling, attempting to straighten your knee. Gently pull your thigh closer to your body while maintaining proper alignment. In this position, flex and extend your foot and knee and rotate your ankle; this increases ankle flexibility. The non-stretching leg should be fully extended on the floor to achieve the maximum stretch (see the first precaution below). Repeat the stretch with your other leg.

PRECAUTIONS

- If the fully extended leg position is uncomfortable for you, bend your nonstretching leg, placing the sole of your foot on the floor.
- Pay attention to the alignment of your neck and shoulders; they often tense up in this position.
- Keep your hips and lower back in contact with the floor.

FIGURE 6-24 The knee-bend stretch

The Cobra Stretch

The cobra (Figure 6-25) is a position derived from yoga. Its arching position balances the forward bending of the previous stretches. Lying flat on the floor on your stomach, place your palms on the floor, next to your shoulders. Beginning at the bottom of your thoracic spine, arch backward while slowly straightening your arms. If you have no history of misalignment in your cervical spine, lift your chin and look toward the ceiling; if you have neck or back problems, do not rise higher than your elbows. Your hipbones should remain in contact with the floor. Slowly bend your arms to roll your chest down to the starting position.

FIGURE 6-25 The cobra stretch

FIGURE 6-26 The chest lift

PRECAUTIONS

- (For the cobra stretch, page 83) tighten the abdominal muscles to avoid unnecessary strain to your lower back.
- Do not let your head drop back.
- Straighten your arms only to the point where the stretch feels comfortable, not painful.
- Avoid overarching your lower back, which overstresses your lumbar spine.

The Chest Lift

The chest lift (Figure 6-26) increases flexibility in the chest and fluidity in the movement of the spine. Lie on your back with your lower back pressed against the floor and your arms in second position. As your torso is initially lifted from the floor, do not let your head come forward. Allow your head to follow your torso; your chest initiates the action. Lift your torso to a sitting position, leading with your upper chest and with your arms trailing. Reach toward your feet. Avoid rounding your upper back by pressing forward with your lower back and tilting your pelvis forward. Reverse the movement by contracting your spine sequentially, beginning with your pelvis and curling down to the original flat-back position.

PRECAUTION

- Avoid rounding your back on the sitting reach toward your feet; rounding puts too much stress on the sciatic nerve.

STRENGTH-BUILDING EXERCISES

In most jazz dance classes, exercises are performed to increase the strength of the abdominal muscles, as well as the chest and arm muscles.

Abdominals

Before exercises to tone and strengthen the abdominals are described, it is important to understand how this group of muscles works. The main muscle of the abdominal region is the long sheath called the *rectus abdominus,* which attaches at the ribs at one end and the pubic bone at the other end. Whenever this muscle contracts, which happens when the spine is flexed or bent, the entire muscle shortens. There are exercises that put more stress on the upper third or lower third of the muscle, but in reality the entire muscle contracts. Therefore, if someone says, "This exercise works the lower abdominals," it must be understood that there are no lower abdominals; the exercise is merely putting emphasis on the lower region.

The *oblique abdominal* muscles run across the rib cage and attach to the edges of the pubic bone. There is one on each side of the body. Their function is to rotate the spine. These muscles are activated when the trunk is twisted or rotated.

The last abdominal muscle is a deep muscle that lies under the *rectus abdominus* and the obliques. This muscle, called the *transverse abdominal,* is used mainly for posture. If good alignment is maintained (see Chapter 3), this muscle group will maintain its tone.

Ways to make abdominal exercises more difficult are:

1. Change the arm positions (farther from the body is harder).
2. Lift the torso higher from the ground.
3. Perform each exercise at a slower pace.

It is also necessary to maintain tension in the abdominals at all times. The head should never return completely to the floor. If the abdominal muscle relaxes, the maximum benefits from the exercise are not achieved.

The Half Sit-Up or Curl-Up   Lie on your back, clasping your hands behind your head. Keep your elbows back. Bend your knees, placing the soles of your feet firmly on the floor. Press your lower back to the floor and contract the abdominals. Exhale while sitting up halfway and maintaining the abdominal contraction (Figure 6-27). Let your hands support the weight of your head, and keep the abdominals tight throughout the exercise. Inhale while lowering and keep your shoulders off the floor throughout the exercise.

FIGURE 6-27 The half sit-up or curl-up

PRECAUTIONS

- To avoid use of your lower back in all half sit-up positions, press down the abdominals, keeping the sacrum on the floor before lifting your shoulders.
- Never perform abdominal work in a straight-leg position, which could strain your lower back.
- When performing all half sit-ups, avoid pulling forward on your neck.
- If the abdominal muscles start to quiver or if you feel yourself jerking to get up, stop. These are signs that the abdominal muscles are tired; you are likely to lose the correct position, possibly causing lower back damage.

Variations

- Hands to reach to knees
- Hands crossed at the chest
- One leg to the ceiling (Figure 6-28)
- Both legs to the ceiling and crossed at the ankles (Figure 6-29)
- Legs to the ceiling and slightly spread apart

FIGURE 6-28 Variation: One leg up

FIGURE 6-29 Variation: Both legs up and crossed

FIGURE 6-30 The abdominal curl

FIGURE 6-31 The abdominal curl-down

The Abdominal Curl Lie on your back, bend your legs, clasp your hands behind your head, and keep your elbows back. Contract the abdominals and press your lower back to the floor. Simultaneously exhale, lift your bent legs off the floor, and lift your head and shoulders until your elbows touch your knees. Inhale and release your torso slightly away from your knees, but do not return to the floor. Figure 6-30 shows the sequence of movements. Take the precautions recommended for the half sit-up. Make sure that when you lift your knees, you are lifting your hips off the ground as well. Do not use momentum to lift your hips!

The Abdominal Curl-Down Begin in a sitting position with your knees bent and your feet flat on the floor. Relax your arms, palms up, at the sides of your body. Slowly lower your torso to the floor by rounding your back, contracting the abdominal muscles, and placing one vertebra at a time on the floor. Do not hold your breath. End by lying flat on the floor. Figure 6-31 shows the sequence of movements. This is an effective transition for lowering your spine to the floor.

The Oblique Curl Start in the same position as the curl-up, but reach your left arm out to the side on the floor. Lift your right elbow and your chest diagonally toward your left knee. Lower until only your head is off the ground and then repeat. Repeat on the other side (Figure 6-32).

FIGURE 6-32 Oblique curl

Variations

- One leg to ceiling and opposite hand touches toes of opposite foot
- Both knees to chest and both hands behind head and touch opposite elbow to opposite knee in a bicycle motion
- Legs to ceiling and crossed at ankles, hands behind head, and touch opposite elbow to opposite knee

Side Bends   Start in the same position as the curl-up but with your hands at the side on the floor. With your right hand, reach as far to your right ankle as possible. Repeat with the left side. Your head is lifted off the floor for the entire exercise, and your hands stay close to the ground (Figure 6-33).

Arm Strength

Most jazz dance classes will incorporate push-ups as a means to develop upper body strength. Strength in the arms and upper body is required of the dancer for balance and for turning and jumping technique. Additionally, dancers must be able to support their body weight in falls and floorwork.

FIGURE 6-33 Side bends

FIGURE 6-34 The modified push-up

The Modified Push-Up Push-ups strengthen the triceps and pectoral muscles. Beginners or students with weak wrists should do the modified push-up rather than the full push-up. The modified is easier because the arms do not bear the full weight of the torso. Place padding under the knees.

Lie facedown on the floor. Place your hands under your shoulders, with fingers facing forward. Keep your feet together, legs bent at the knees. Keep your body in one plane from knees to head while pushing your upper body off the floor. Contract the abdominals and hip muscles, press your knees together, and tighten your buttocks to prevent your back from sagging. Continue pushing until your arms are almost straight; leaving a slight bend in your elbows prevents joint strain. Figure 6-34 shows the upward movement. Lower your body so that your chest almost touches the floor, and keep your body in one plane.

PRECAUTIONS

- Make sure your body is in one plane from your knees to the tip of your head.
- Do not keep your arms straight when you lower. Your arms must bend or they are not doing the work.
- Do not hold your breath.

The Push-Up Lie facedown on the floor. Place your hands under your shoulders, with fingers facing forward. Keep your feet together and flexed, with the weight on the balls of your feet. Push your body off the floor, contracting the abdominals and hip muscles and tightening your buttocks to keep your back from sagging. Keeping your body in one plane,

FIGURE 6-35 The push-up

push up until your arms are almost straight; leaving a slight bend in your elbows prevents joint strain. Figure 6-35 shows the upward movement. Lower your body so that your chest almost touches the floor by bending your elbows, keeping the weight equally distributed on your hands and the balls of your feet.

PRECAUTIONS

- To prevent back strain, do not let your lower back sag.
- Do not raise your buttocks to dip your chin.

BODY ISOLATIONS

Body isolations are the trademark of jazz dance, and the student should master them early in training. A body isolation is the movement of only one part of the body. Isolations generally take place at the head, shoulders, ribs, and hips.

FIGURE 6-36 Some head isolations. Do not tip the head back farther than 2 inches.

The Head

Head isolations (Figure 6-36) are performed by turning the head to the right, left, chin down, chin up, laterally from shoulder to shoulder, and by extending the head forward and backward. The head can also rotate in a complete circle. Students with a history of cervical misalignment or chronic fatigue in the neck should limit their range of motion when dropping the head forward, backward, or to the side. Looseness in the neck is essential for head isolations.

PRECAUTION

- Do not let your head drop all the way back. This may strain the cervical vertebrae.

The Shoulders

The shoulders can elevate, depress, rotate forward and backward, and make a complete circle. The shoulders can isolate so that one shoulder can move at a time or so that both can move in the same direction or opposite directions. Figure 6-37 shows some shoulder isolations.

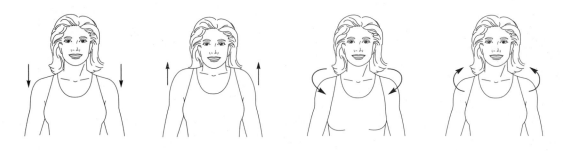

FIGURE 6-37 Some shoulder isolations

The Ribs

The ribs are probably the hardest part of the body to isolate because in our daily life this isolation is rarely executed. The ribs can shift from side to side and can push forward and backward. The ribs can also rotate in a circle. Figure 6-38 shows some rib isolations. Isolations of the ribs are easier to learn in a sitting position because the hips are stabilized.

The Hips

The hips (Figure 6-39), like the ribs, move side to side, forward and backward, and in a complete circle. It is easier to move the hips in *plié* because the position allows the ligaments of the hips to loosen.

When performing isolation movements, remember to do just that—isolate. Pay special attention to keeping the shoulders still when moving the neck and keeping the hips still when moving the ribs. The mastery of these simple isolations will lead to *polycentrics,* or the combining of iso-

FIGURE 6-38 Some rib isolations

FIGURE 6-39 Some hip isolations

lated parts. For example, a skilled dancer can move the head in one direction while the shoulders isolate in another direction, the hips circle,
and the hands create a flashy, explosive pattern.

Another way to add complexity is to move these isolations through
space. Many instructors have students perform the isolations while performing a jazz walk, a *chassé,* or a run. It is fun to do a pivot turn while
swinging the head or doing a jazz walk in a circle with shoulder shrugs as
an accent. Hip rolls or rib cage isolations while doing a jazz walk or strut
are other examples of incorporating isolation exercises with locomotor
movements. The possibilities for practicing isolations while performing
locomotor movements are numerous. The use of isolation and locomotor movements in combination is one of the trademarks of jazz dance.

BALANCE EXERCISES

At the conclusion of the warm-up, balance exercises are often performed.
Because balance is the key to success in many dance movements, balance
must be practiced to achieve consistency and skill. Outlined below are exercises to improve your balance technique. These exercises can be performed at the barre.

Exercise 1   *Relevé* in first position (Figure 6-40). While still in *relevé,*
transfer all weight onto your right leg, bringing your left foot to *coupé*
position. (The *coupé* is described in Chapter 4). After four or eight
counts, return to *relevé* on both legs. Transfer your weight onto your left
leg with your right foot in the *coupé* position.

FIGURE 6-40

Exercise 2   Begin as in exercise 1, but while in *coupé* position, lower the supporting leg to a flat foot in four counts (Figure 6-41). Return to *relevé* in four counts. Repeat four times on the right side before executing the exercise on the left side.

Exercise 3   Begin as in exercise 1, but while in *coupé*, *plié-relevé* on the supporting leg (Figure 6-42). Return to *relevé* on both legs. Repeat the exercise on your left leg.

Exercise 4   Begin as in exercise 1, to *coupé* position. In *relevé* extend the *coupé* leg to the side and hold this balance for eight counts (Figure 6-43). Repeat the exercise on your other leg.

FIGURE 6-41

FIGURE 6-42   FIGURE 6-43

Exercise 5 This final exercise (Figure 6-44) should not be attempted until the dancer has mastered the single *pirouette*. Begin in a parallel fourth position, with your back heel lifted off the ground and your arms extended to second position. On counts 1 and 2, kick-ball change with your back foot. (The kick-ball change is discussed in Chapter 7). On count 3, bring your back foot to parallel *passé* and simultaneously *relevé* on the supporting leg. Bend your arms in so that your hands are in front of your chest. On count 4, balance in this position. Repeat this exercise four times, then perform it by making quarter turns as you *passé*. Repeat the exercise, making half turns. Repeat again, making full turns as you bring the leg to *passé*. When you can competently execute single turns, attempt multiple turns.

FIGURE 6-44

Barry Lather in an instructional video for street dance. Lather has choreographed for stars such as Paula Abdul, Janet Jackson, Michael Jackson, George Michael, the artist formerly known as Prince, and Sting.

CHAPTER 7

BASIC JAZZ DANCE

This chapter describes movements used during floor and combination sections of the jazz dance class. Dance steps are listed in order of difficulty. Often, the learning of one step may assist in the learning of another. When attempting these movements on your own, pay particular attention to posture and observe the movement tips listed. When you can successfully perform these steps, you'll discover that you really are dancing!

LOCOMOTOR MOVEMENTS

Most locomotor movements use the arms in some way. The arms and legs are often coordinated in opposition. *Opposition* means that the opposite arm and leg are forward during a step; for example, in the *chassé*, the right foot steps out on the first step and the left arm extends forward. The same is true for jazz walks; when the left foot steps forward, the right arm is forward. In a typical fan kick with the right leg, the left arm sweeps overhead in the opposite direction (the fan kick is discussed later in this section).

Jazz Walks

There are many varieties of jazz walks. Jazz walks can be performed in *plié* (Figure 7-1), in *relevé* (Figure 7-2), in *plié-relevé* (Figures 7-3 and 7-4), with isolation movements, in any direction, and at any tempo. The technique for the basic jazz walk is to roll through the ball of the foot and then lower the heel to the floor. The legs stretch and reach as far as possible, and at least one foot maintains contact with the floor at all times. The jazz walk is stylized with a step longer than the natural stride. Another stylized variation of the jazz walk is the strut (Figure 7-5). Between each step of this movement, the leg comes through a low *passé* position.

FIGURE 7-1 Jazz walk in plié

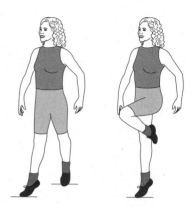

FIGURE 7-2
Jazz walk in
relevé

FIGURE 7-3
Jazz walk in
plié-relevé

FIGURE 7-4 Jazz
walk in *plié-relevé*
with *passé*

FIGURE 7-5 Strut

MOVEMENT TIPS

- Do not change the level of bounce when doing a jazz walk; keep it fluid.
- Do not place your heel down first when stepping.

The Step Touch

The step touch (Figure 7-6) is a progression from the walk. This movement can travel forward, backward, or sideward. Start by stepping to the front, back, or side of the supporting leg. The opposite foot touches the floor; no weight is placed on the foot. Generally, the touch is done with the ball of the foot, without the heel touching the floor. A touch may be done with the leg straight or bent; the touch may be to the front, back, or side of the stepping foot. A touch is sometimes referred to as a dig.

MOVEMENT TIP

- Do not put weight on the foot that performs the touch.

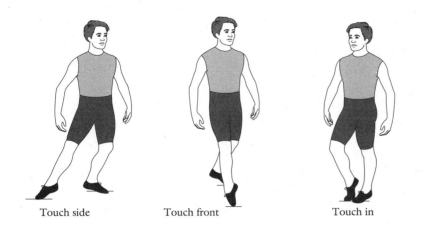

Touch side   Touch front   Touch in

FIGURE 7-6 The step touch

The Cross Touch

The cross touch (Figure 7-7) is another walk and touch progression. This movement can travel forward or backward. Start by stepping across in a *demi-plié*. The opposite foot touches the floor to the side or second position.

The Camel Walk

This is a very stylized walk using the torso movement of the body wave (Figure 7-8). Step forward with the heel of the lead foot. Roll from the heel onto the ball of the foot while at the same time executing a body wave upward from the lower back and hips. Finish with the opposite foot sliding in to meet the stepping foot.

FIGURE 7-7 The cross touch   FIGURE 7-8 Camel walk

FIGURE 7-9 The jazz square

The Jazz Square

The jazz square consists of four walking steps performed in a square (Figure 7-9). The first step travels forward, the second crosses in front of the first, the third step travels backward, and the fourth step opens to the side. The hips and arms are usually used in this step to stylize and accent the movements.

The Jazz Slide

The jazz slide is initiated by stepping to a turned-out second-position lunge and sliding the straight leg along the floor, foot pointed (Figure 7-10). The hip of the bent leg is pushed in the direction of the lunge so

FIGURE 7-10 The jazz slide

that the body is tilted and asymmetrical. The arms are in second position but, because the body is tilted, they are on an oblique line parallel to the extended sliding leg.

MOVEMENT TIP

• Do not put weight on the straight extended leg.

The Grapevine

The grapevine (Figure 7-11) is another variation on a walk. This movement travels to the side and can be performed at various tempos. Begin by stepping to the right with the right foot. Step with the left, crossing behind your right foot. Step to the right with the right foot. Step with the left, crossing in front of your right foot. The hips can twist with the movement or they can remain stable. The grapevine can be performed in *plié* or *relevé*. As you progress, you can perform these four steps in a turning pattern.

The Chassé

Chassé ("chase") is a term borrowed from ballet, where it is defined as a slide. In jazz it is also a sliding movement, but on closer examination, it

FIGURE 7-11 The grapevine

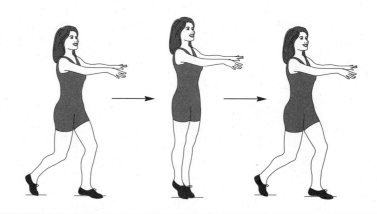

FIGURE 7-12a The *chassé*—on the floor

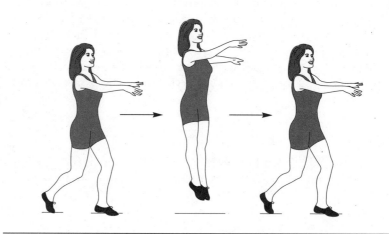

FIGURE 7-12b The *chassé*—in the air

can be analyzed as a step-together-step (Figure 7-12a). It is a movement that travels forward, backward, or sideward. When performed to its fullest, it brings the dancer into the air (Figure 7-12b). When in the air, the legs should be straight, feet pointed and crossed in a tight fifth position. It can be counted as one-and-two.

The Kick-Ball Change

The **kick-ball change** is a step derived from tap dance. This step is counted one-and-two and is regularly used as a transition step because it

FIGURE 7-13 The kick-ball change

involves little or no traveling. One leg kicks as high as determined by flexibility or choreography. The kicking leg steps to the rear of the supporting leg, placing the weight on the ball of the foot, heel lifted. The other foot then steps in place with the weight changing or transferring onto this foot; hence the name *kick-ball change.* Figure 7-13 shows the movement sequence.

The *Pas de Bourrée*

The *pas de bourrée* ("*bourrée* step," a movement from a seventeenth-century French dance) is a ballet step consisting of three steps. The jazz *pas de bourrée* can be performed in several ways. It also can be counted in several ways: one-and-two-, one-and-ah, two-and-ah. The count depends on the tempo and the accent (see Chapter 9).

The *Pas de Bourrée* in Place or Traveling Forward or Backward *The pas de bourrée* in place or traveling forward or backward begins in second position. The first step crosses in front or back. In the second step, the opposite foot steps to second position. In the third step, the first foot steps in place. This *pas de bourrée* may be referred to as "cross, side, front." Figure 7-14 shows the movement sequence.

The *Pas de Bourrée* Traveling Sideward In *pas de bourrées* traveling sideward, the first step crosses in back. The second step travels to second position. The third step crosses over the second step, traveling farther sideward. This *pas de bourrée* may be referred to as "back, side, front." Figure 7-15 shows the movement sequence. After you learn this step, you can attempt the *pas de bourrée* turning.

FIGURE 7-14 The *pas de bourrée* traveling forward

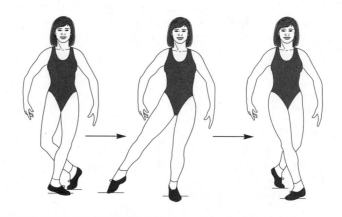

FIGURE 7-15 The *pas de bourrée* traveling sideward

MOVEMENT TIPS

- In all *pas de bourrées* make sure to continually shift the weight from one foot to the other.
- Do not let the weight shift back onto your heels.

| Preparation | Step back | Turn | Cross front |

FIGURE 7-16 The *pas de bourrée* turning

The *Pas de Bourrée* Turning As in the *pas de bourrée* traveling side-ward, the first step crosses in back. The second step turns the body halfway around by stepping toward the back. The third step completes the turn by crossing in front of the second step. Figure 7–16 shows the movement sequence.

The Triplet

The triplet (Figure 7-17) is a three-step movement, with the first step in *plié* and the second and third steps in *relevé*. It usually travels forward but can also travel backward, to the side, or turning. It can be counted in measures of threes or as one-and-two. A triplet may be identified as a mamba when it is executed with a twisting of the torso and hips.

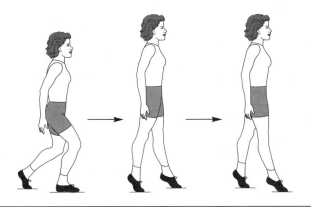

FIGURE 7-17 The triplet

Relevé   *Plié-relevé*

FIGURE 7-18 Kicks

Kicks *(Grand Battements)*

Kicks, or *grand battements* (Figure 7-18), can be performed in place as
described in the ballet chapter (Chapter 4), or they can be performed
while traveling across the floor. To perform the kick as a traveling movement, step in front of the kicking leg and then kick the leg that is free.
Repeat this step across the floor. When doing this movement, the supporting leg can be flat-footed or in *plié, relevé,* or *plié-relevé* (often termed
"forced arch" because of the exaggerated, or forced, arch of the foot).
The extended leg, the leg that is kicking, may be straight or developed.
Developed means the leg goes through a *passé* position (described in
Chapter 4) and then is extended to a high kick.

MOVEMENT TIPS

- Contract the abdominal muscles to avoid unnecessary strain on
  your lower back.
- Do not let your chest collapse when you are extending your leg.
  Keep your chest and spine well lifted and elongated.
- Do not elevate your shoulders.
- Depress your shoulders to keep your torso erect and arm move-
  ment controlled.
- Do not tilt your pelvis when kicking; maintain the horizontal
  line between the pelvic bones.

FIGURE 7-19 The fan kick

The Fan Kick

In the fan kick, the leg makes a sweeping arc through space. It crosses in front of the body, then sweeps to make a half circle before touching the ground. Figure 7-19 shows the movement sequence. The sweeping leg can be either straight or in *attitude;* ideally, the leg should be at hip level. The supporting leg can be in *plié, relevé,* or *relevé* with a bent knee (termed *plié-relevé*).

PRECAUTIONS

- Do not attempt this movement unless your hip and leg muscles are fully warmed up.
- This is an advanced kicking movement. Do not attempt it until your teacher has affirmed that your kicking technique is correct.

Turns

Turns are rotating movements performed in place or traveling. They are executed by turning the whole body on two feet, on one foot, from one foot to the other, or while jumping. Remember that the secret to successful turns is spotting.

The Pivot Turn

The pivot turn is a turn on two feet. Begin by stepping forward on one foot. Quickly change the direction of your body to face the opposite direction. Both feet remain in contact with the floor when the pivot is executed. To make a full, or complete, pivot turn, step forward again but in a line opposite from the original direction (Figure 7-20). Continue the pivot to end up facing in the original direction. Remember to spot.

MOVEMENT TIPS

- Keep your body weight fully on the balls of your feet.
- Make sure the turn is sharp.

The Paddle Turn

The paddle turn is a simple turn that pivots the body around one spot. The weight is continually shifted from one foot to the other. The sup-

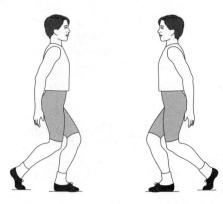

FIGURE 7-20 The pivot turn

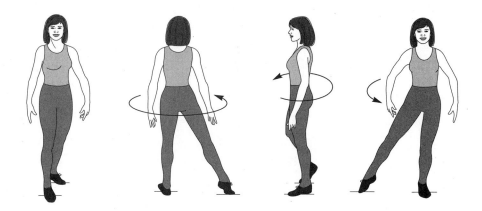

FIGURE 7-21 The paddle turn

porting stationary leg pivots on the ball of the foot, with the heel lifting slightly off the floor. The other leg is extended to the side and "paddles" on the ball of the foot, rotating the body in a circular direction while the foot traces an imaginary circular pattern on the floor (Figure 7-21).

MOVEMENT TIP

- To get exact quarter turns, imagine a clock on the floor. The "paddle" foot must touch at 12 o'clock, 3 o'clock, 6 o'clock, and 9 o'clock.

The *Chaîné* Turn

Chaîné ("chained") turns derive from ballet but are also included in jazz dance. A *chaîné* turn is a two-step turn generally performed in *relevé*, but it may also be performed in *plié*. The body rotates 180 degrees on each step of the turn, and the turning movement progresses in a straight line. The weight shifts from one leg to the other with evenly balanced steps. In *chaîné* turns performed in *relevé*, the legs should be held in first position turned out. In *chaîné* turns performed in *plié*, the legs may be held parallel or turned out in either first or second position. Figure 7-22 shows a typical position for the *chaîné* turn.

FIGURE 7-22 The *chaîné* turn

MOVEMENT TIPS

- Pay particular attention to posture. Do not overextend your rib cage.
- Spotting is necessary.
- When you first begin to learn the *chaîné* turn, place your arms on your shoulders so they do not distract you.

The *Soutenu* Turn

The *soutenu* ("sustained") turn also originates in ballet. In jazz, the *soutenu* turn may rotate in quarter turns, half turns, or whole turns. Prepare for the turn by stepping to parallel second in *plié*, pulling the second leg in to meet the preparation leg as the turn is executed with both legs in *relevé*. The weight of the body is shared equally by both legs during the turn. Figure 7-23 shows a *soutenu* full turn. The turn may be executed either inward or outward, with the second leg being pulled in, to cross either in front or in back of the preparation leg.

The Touch Turn

The touch turn (Figure 7-24) is a variation of the *soutenu* turn. Rather than the weight being shared by both legs, the turn is executed partially

FIGURE 7-23 The *soutenu* full turn

FIGURE 7-24 The touch turn

around on one leg as the opposite leg touches the floor. To complete the turn, the weight transfers to the "touching" leg by stepping onto that foot. The touch turn, or touch *soutenu,* can be executed in either *relevé* or *plié.*

The *Pirouette*

The *pirouette* ("whirling about") is a ballet turn performed in place, with one leg in *relevé* and the other in *passé* (Figure 7-25). The *pirouette* may be performed in parallel or turned-out position. Parallel *pirouettes* may also be done with the supporting leg in *plié.* In performing *pirouettes,* bring the lifted knee directly to high *passé,* maintain good alignment, and spot.

En dehors   *En dedans*

FIGURE 7-25 The *pirouette*

Pirouettes are important turns in jazz dance. They are also a continual challenge for a jazz dancer of any level. *Pirouettes* take time and practice. As your dance skill progresses, you will graduate from doing half turns to full turns to multiple turns.

En dehors and *en dedans* are two terms used when describing *pirouettes*. *En dehors* means "outward." It indicates that a *pirouette* turns out from the supporting leg. An easy way to remember the meaning of *en dehors* is to think of the phrase "*out* the door." *En dedans* means "inward." It indicates that the nonsupporting leg turns into the supporting leg.

The *Piqué* Turn

The *piqué* ("point") turn is another turn borrowed from ballet. It is a full turn performed turned out in *relevé* on one foot and progresses in a straight line. Prepare for the turn with one leg in *demi-plié* and the other leg straight forward. Begin the turn by stepping sideward with the straight leg in *relevé*. The opposite leg closes to a low *passé* position behind the knee of the straight leg during the turn. The turn ends in the preparation position, and the straight leg then steps sideward again to execute the next turn. Figure 7-26 shows the movement sequence. It is important to extend the leg fully when stepping into *relevé* and to step directly under the straight leg when coming to *plié* from the *passé* position.

MOVEMENT TIP

- To learn this turn, try the movement without turning. Practice just the *piqué* movement of stepping directly into the *relevé* position with the extended leg and bringing the other leg to *passé*. When this can be done successfully, attempt to execute the turn.

FIGURE 7-26 The *piqué* turn

AERIAL MOVEMENTS

Aerial movements are any unsupported or "in the air" movements. Aerial movements include jumps, hops, and leaps. Aerial movements are generally categorized as the following movements:

Taking off from two feet and landing on two feet

Taking off from two feet and landing on one foot

Taking off from one foot and landing on two feet

Taking off from one foot and landing on the other foot

The principles of jumping outlined in Chapter 4 should be followed for all aerial movements not only to help achieve correct technique but also to help reduce injury risk. This section describes jazz jumps, hops, leaps, and their variations.

Jumps

Jumps are aerial movements that take off from two feet and land on two feet. There are several variations that may be used in jazz dance classes.

The Straight Jump   Begin in *demi-plié*. Jump straight up into the air, keeping your body tight and correctly aligned. Land on both feet, rolling through the balls of your feet and into *demi-plié* (Figure 7-27).

The Arch Jump   Begin in *demi-plié*. Jump straight up into the air. At the height of the jump, arch your upper back. At the same time, lift both legs to the rear, keeping them straight. Land on both feet, rolling through the balls of your feet and into *demi-plié* (Figure 7-28).

FIGURE 7-27 The straight jump

FIGURE 7-28 The arch jump

FIGURE 7-29 The pike jump   FIGURE 7-30 The tuck jump

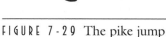

The Pike Jump   Begin in *demi-plié*. Jump straight up into the air. At the height of the jump, "pike" your body (torso flexion) at your hips. At the same time, bring both legs forward, keeping them straight. Land on both feet, rolling through the balls of your feet and into *demi-plié* (Figure 7-29).

The Tuck Jump   Begin in *demi-plié*. Jump straight up into the air. At the height of the jump, bring both knees together toward your chest, keeping your back and torso straight and correctly aligned. Land on both feet, rolling through the balls of your feet and into *demi-plié* (Figure 7-30).

The Hop

A hop is an aerial movement that takes off on one foot and lands on that same foot. Variations exist as they do with all jumps. A popular jazz hop is the *passé* hop with the lifted leg in high *passé* (Figure 7-31).

The *Assemblé*

Assemblé is a ballet term meaning "assembled." It is any aerial movement that starts on either one foot or both feet and ends with both feet together (Figure 7-32).

FIGURE 7-31 The *passé* hop

FIGURE 7-32 The *assemblé*

The *Sissonne*

The *sissonne* (named for the originator of the step) is a ballet jump that takes off from both feet and lands on one foot, with the other leg lifted in the air (Figure 7-33). The lifted leg may end in any position desired: *attitude* side, front, or back; *battement* front or side; *arabesque;* or *passé*.

The Catleap

The catleap was taken from the ballet movement *pas de chat,* meaning paw of the cat. In jazz, the catleap is performed with the legs in parallel

FIGURE 7-33 The *sissonne*

FIGURE 7-34 The catleap

front *attitude* (Figure 7-34). The catleap begins with a lunge forward to a *demi-plié*. The rear leg is then brought forward to the parallel front *attitude*. As the body rises in the air, the legs exchange *attitude* positions. The first leg forward in the front *attitude* becomes the landing support.

The Hitch Kick

In the hitch kick, the legs pass each other in a scissorlike fashion in the air; the first kicking leg becomes the landing support leg. Jazz dance uses several variations of the hitch kick.

The Hitch Kick Forward   The hitch kick forward begins with a lunge forward to a *demi-plié*. The rear leg is then kicked forward. As the body rises in the air, the legs pass in scissorlike fashion as the second leg is also kicked forward. The landing is on the first kicking leg in a *demi-plié*, with the second kicking leg still held high. The kicking legs are held straight throughout. Figure 7-35 shows the movement sequence. The hitch kick forward may also be done from the lunge with the first kicking leg bent and the second kicking leg straight (Figure 7-36).

The Hitch Kick to the Rear   The hitch kick to the rear begins with a lunge onto one leg in *demi-plié*. The rear leg is then kicked backward. As the body rises in the air, the legs pass in scissorlike fashion as the second leg is also kicked backward. The landing is on the first kicking leg in a

FIGURE 7-35 The hitch kick forward

FIGURE 7-36 The hitch kick forward with the first leg bent

demi-plié, with the second kicking leg held high in an *arabesque.* The kicking legs are held straight throughout. Figure 7-37 shows the movement sequence.

FIGURE 7-37 The hitch kick to the rear

The *Jeté*

The *jeté* is the grandest leap. It is a large jump from one foot to the other, in which the legs create the vision of an arc in the air. At its fullest, the *jeté* is done with the legs in a split position in the air. There are, however, many variations of the *jeté* or grand leap. The *jeté* may be done by executing a *developé* (an extension of the leg through the *passé* position) into a split position or the stag position (one leg bent and one leg straight). Figure 7-38 shows the *jeté*.

FIGURE 7-38 Example of the *jeté*

MOVEMENT TIPS

- Do not look at the floor; focus out and slightly above the level you are leaping.
- When performing a straight-leg *jeté*, do not let your back leg bend. Push off the floor to fully extend your back leg.
- A helpful preparatory exercise for leaps: Execute a *grand battement* with your front leg, then immediately step onto that leg to execute a *grand battement* to the back with the opposite leg.

PRECAUTIONS

- Make sure to land in *plié* to avoid unnecessary strain on your knee.
- Keep your torso erect to avoid unnecessary strain on your lower back.

 LOORWORK

Floorwork is an exciting and dynamic aspect of jazz dance. Floorwork skills should be learned in a progressive order and executed slowly with control to reduce risk of injury. Many of the advanced floorwork skills are derived from gymnastics and require precise timing. It is advisable to wear knee pads when first learning skills involving floorwork.

FIGURE 7-39
The cookie sit

The Cookie Sit

The cookie sit, or fourth position on the floor, is a stationary pose. The cookie is a double stag position of the legs while sitting erect. For variations of the cookie position, the upper torso position can be altered (Figure 7-39).

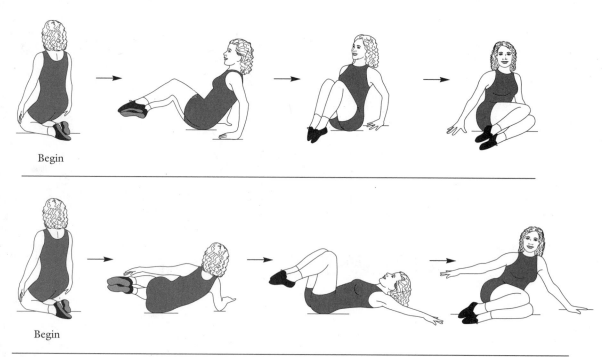

Begin

Begin

FIGURE 7-40 The tuck roll

The Tuck Roll

The tuck position is with both legs together in parallel. It is advisable to learn the tuck roll by first executing this skill in the sitting position before performing it completely on the floor. You may begin this skill in a variety of positions, but for this exercise, begin by sitting in a tuck position on your knees. Sit sideward with the weight on one hip. Progress by rolling through the sitting position with arm support behind your hips, tucking your legs closely to your chest. Continue the tuck roll to the opposite hip. End in the sitting tuck position. To perform the tuck roll completely on the floor, roll onto your back during the tuck position (Figure 7-40).

The Russian or Straddle Roll

The Russian or straddle roll may be performed from a variety of positions on the floor. Begin the Russian roll by sitting in a tuck position as in the tuck roll. Sit sideward with the weight on one hip. Extend your top leg and begin to fan kick as you progress through the sitting position. Continue rolling through the sitting position with arm support behind your hips, straddling your legs (that is, extending the legs in second position).

FIGURE 7-41 The Russian or straddle roll

Roll to the opposite hip while at the same time tucking the initial fan-kick leg. Roll onto the bent knee and then either step onto the second straddle leg or tuck both knees to return to the kneeling position. You may perform the Russian roll completely on the floor by rolling onto your back during the straddle position (Figure 7-41).

ALLS

Falls are interesting methods of changing the dimension of dance movements by quickly dropping the body onto the floor. Although falls are meant to look as though the body is relaxed, in reality, the body must be in strict control. To perform falls, you must learn to isometrically contract the torso muscles and use the muscles of the arms and shoulders to lessen the impact of the fall, cushioning the force through your elbows and hands. Avoid landing or hitting the floor with your knees, elbows, or coccyx; land on the soft parts of your body.

The Knee Fall

Begin in a kneeling position with your arms extended horizontally. Keeping your back straight and the abdominals contracted, fall forward to the prone position. Cushion the "fall" by catching yourself in the push-up position and gently lowering yourself to the floor (Figure 7-42).

The Jazz Split Slide

Begin in fourth position. *Tendu* your front leg, keeping the weight of your body on your rear leg. Your front leg slides forward while your rear leg *pliés*, remaining in a turned-out position. During the slide, your front leg bears little weight as your torso leans slightly to the side of that leg. The arm on the same side as the forward leg reaches to the floor to sup-

FIGURE 7-42 The knee fall

FIGURE 7-43 The jazz split slide

port your body weight and to protect your rear knee as you slide to the half-split position. As you reach the floor, finish the slide in the jazz split position (Figure 7-43).

PRECAUTIONS

- Contract the abdominals so that there is no stress on your lower back.
- Your rear leg must remain turned out so that the top of your knee doesn't hit the floor.
- Your arms should support your body weight; do not fall to the floor.

LOCOMOTOR COMBINATIONS

Once you are familiar with the steps in this chapter, it is time to combine them. Included are sample combinations for you to practice and study. Students and teachers are encouraged to manipulate these combinations by changing their tempos, directions, dimensions, and dynamics (see Chapter 9). See how many combinations can be built from the ones described.

COMBINATION 1

Counts

1	Jazz walk right
2	Jazz walk left
3	Jazz walk right
4	Jazz walk left
5	Step right
6	Half pivot
7	Step right
8	Half pivot

COMBINATION 2

Counts

1	Jazz walk right
2	Jazz walk left
3 & 4	*Pas de bourrée* right
5 & 6	*Pas de bourrée* left
7	*Pirouette* turning right, with right foot in parallel *passé* (*en dehors*)
8	Step right from *pirouette*

This combination alternates sides.

COMBINATION 3

Counts

1 & 2	*Chassé* right
3 & 4	*Chassé* left
5-6-7-8	Jazz square right
1 & 2	Kick-ball change right
3	Fan kick right
4	Step right from fan kick
5-6-7-8	Jazz square left

This combination alternates sides.

COMBINATION 4

Counts

1-2	Step right, hop with left foot in parallel *passé*
3-4	Step left, hop with right foot in parallel *passé*
5-6-7-8	Four jazz walks in a full circle: right, left, right, left
1 & 2	Kick-ball change right
3	Step right
4	Step left into fourth position *demi-plié* (preparation)
5	*Pirouette* turning right, with right foot in parallel *passé* (en dehors)
6	Step right from *pirouette*
7	Step left foot together to parallel first, *demi-plié*
8	Tuck jump; clap on landing

COMBINATION 5

Counts

1-2	*Chaîné* right (right, left)
3	Step right
4	*Tendu* front left
5-6	Jazz split slide to floor
7-8	Cookie sit
1-3	Tuck roll ending on knees
4	Step right to step up to stand
5	Step left to parallel second position, *relevé*, with arms in jazz fifth
& 6	Ball change, right, left, to parallel first position, *demi-plié*. Body contraction with fists pulled to waist
7	Repeat count 5
& 8	Repeat counts & 6

Natasha Baron, New York dancer and choreographer, demonstrates the flexibility needed to be a jazz dancer.

CHAPTER 8

Movements to Challenge the Beginning Dancer

Jazz dance at the beginning level offers a multitude of movement possibilities. The exciting news is that the list of jazz dance steps and movements is never ending. The more you learn, the more there is to know! Included in this chapter are a few additional movements to challenge the advanced beginner dancer. Here are a few more steps to lead you on the path that keeps you hooked on dance!

Turns

Multiple Turns

Once you have experienced each of the turns in Chapter 7, you will want to concentrate even more on technique. Sound body alignment and correct placement are the keys to mastering the art of turning. As you progress, you will want to be able to perform **multiple turns,** that is, a series of turns of the same kind. For example, you want to do three *pirouettes* instead of a single *pirouette*. Correct arm positions and arm control are also essential in achieving multiple turns. Arms should be held in the ballet fifth front or *en avant* position with elbows lifted and an isometric resistance involving the muscles of the upper back and the latissimus dorsi. To execute multiple turns successfully, it is essential that you **spot.** During multiple turns, your head must quickly rotate with each turn and your eyes must spot on a fixed point to maintain balance and control.

The Barrel Turn

Begin in a wide second position. Lunge toward one leg, reaching with the opposite arm toward the lunging leg. Twist your shoulders and torso so that the same arm of the supporting lunge leg can be lifted high and toward the rear. The turn is an outward (*en dehors*) *pirouette* done with the supporting leg in *demi-plié.* The body leans forward to begin the turn and arches during the rotation of the turn. The arms circle during the turn, creating a windmill effect (Figure 8-1).

FIGURE 8-1 The barrel turn

The Drag Turn

The drag turn begins in the same preparation position as the *pirouette en dedans* (Chapter 7, page 111). As you execute the turn, the leg that would normally be the *passé* leg drags on the floor next to the foot of the supporting leg. Drag the foot with the toes pointed under, holding the foot near the arch of the supporting leg (Figure 8-2).

FIGURE 8-2 The drag turn

The Pencil Turn

A pencil turn is a type of *pirouette,* but instead of the nonsupporting leg being held in the *passé* position, the turn is executed with both legs straight and the nonsupporting leg pulled tightly alongside the supporting leg. The arms are usually pulled straight against the sides of the body. The dancer appears to have only one leg and can be imagined as a pencil spinning on its point (Figure 8-3).

UMPS

The *Tour en L'air*

The *tour en l'air* is a jump with a 360-degree turn in the air. Begin in a two-foot preparation. At the height of the jump, perform a 360-degree turn *en dehors* (Figure 8-4). It is important to follow the rules of jumping technique and turning and spotting technique described in Chapter 4.

The Straddle Toe Touch

The straddle toe touch may begin from a two-foot preparation or may be linked to a series of leaps. At the height of the jump, lean your chest forward and rotate your hips slightly back as you straddle your legs as wide as possible. Reach sideward with both arms to touch your toes (Figure 8-5).

FIGURE 8-3 The pencil turn

FIGURE 8-4 The *tour en l'air*

FIGURE 8-5 The straddle toe touch

The Double *Attitude* or Stag Leap

Begin from a two-foot jump preparation. At the height of the jump, lift one leg to front *attitude* and one leg to rear *attitude* (Figure 8-6).

FIGURE 8-6 The double *attitude* or stag leap

FIGURE 8-7 The *passé* hop with tuck

H OPS

Passé Hop with Tuck

Perform the basic *passé* hop as described in Chapter 7. At the height of the hop, tuck the supporting leg into the chest parallel and as even to the *passé* leg as possible. Extend the tucked leg prior to the landing. As with the basic *passé* hop, land on the same foot as the take-off foot (Figure 8-7).

The *Passé* Hop with 360-Degree Turn

Perform the basic *passé* hop as described in Chapter 7. At the height of the hop, execute a 360-degree turn *en dedans* (Figure 8-8).

FIGURE 8-8 The *passé* hop with 360-degree turn

FIGURE 8-9 The hitch kick to the side

LEAPS

The Hitch Kick to the Side

The hitch kick to the side begins with a sideward lunge into a *demi-plié*. The trailing leg follows with a straight kick to the side in the direction of movement, crossing over the bent leg. As the body rises in the air, the legs pass in scissorlike fashion as the second leg opens in a straight kick to the side. The landing is on the first kicking leg, quickly followed by the second kicking leg to end in fourth-position *demi-plié*. Figure 8-9 shows the movement sequence.

PRECAUTIONS

- This is an intermediate-level movement, so attempt it cautiously until you understand the technique.
- Contract your abdominal muscles to avoid unnecessary strain on your lower back.
- Do not let your chest collapse when scissoring your legs.
- Do not elevate your shoulders. Depress your shoulders to keep your torso erect and arm movements controlled.

The Back Stag Leap

The back stag leap is a more difficult variation of the grand *jeté* or split leap. At the height of the leap, the rear leg is lifted to a back *attitude*. At its fullest, the toe of the *attitude* is extended as near to the head as possible (Figure 8-10).

FIGURE 8-10 The back stag leap

The Double Split *Jeté*

Begin the double split *jeté* as though you are going to execute a grand *jeté* or split leap. At the height of the jump, exchange your legs in scissorlike fashion so that the rear leg becomes the forward leg of the split leap. Land the double split *jeté* on the new front split leg, which was the take-off leg (Figure 8-11).

FIGURE 8-11 The double split *jeté*

FIGURE 8-12 The knee spin

*F*LOORWORK

The Knee Spin

Begin in a kneeling position. Bring one leg up with your foot on the floor. Execute a 360-degree spin, bringing your legs together during the spin. At the end of the turn, bring the opposite leg up with your foot on the floor (Figure 8-12). Assist the spinning motion as in any *pirouette;* that is, begin with open arms and close your arms to fifth front during the turn. Remember to spot.

The Knee Slide

Begin in a parallel first or second position. Lifting your hips through a hinge position (see Chapter 5, page 65), slide onto your knees. Keep your abdominals and hips tight, and allow your body to slide forward, continuing to lift your hips to avoid a downward fall onto your knees. Raising your arms and chest can assist in maintaining a lifted position during the slide (Figure 8-13).

FIGURE 8-13 The knee slide

FIGURE 8-14 The
front fall

ALLS

The Front Fall

Begin in a parallel first position with your arms extended horizontally from your chest. Keeping your back straight and abdominals contracted, fall forward to the prone position. Cushion the "fall" by catching yourself in the push-up position and gently lowering yourself to the floor (Figure 8-14).

The Swedish Fall

Begin with one leg extended to the rear *arabesque* position. Execute a front fall as described above, while keeping the *arabesque* leg held as high as possible. In this fall, as you catch yourself, cushion the fall by arching your upper back and then lower yourself gently to the floor (Figure 8-15).

FIGURE 8-15 The
Swedish fall

Begin

The Backward Fall

Begin this fall on one leg with the opposite leg in rear *coupé* or rear *passé*. Lower your body onto the floor by placing the top of the foot of the *coupé/passé* leg to the floor a few inches behind the supporting leg. Continue lowering your body as the weight is shifted to the top of your foot. The knee of the *coupé/passé* leg is turned out to avoid any risk of injury. The torso leans slightly forward while the hips rotate back. As your body reaches the floor, curl your torso down until you are lying flat (Figure 8-16).

The Sideward Fall

The sideward fall begins with a sideward lunge into a *demi-plié*. The opposite leg is *entente* behind the supporting leg with the toe pointed under. Lower your body to the floor by sliding your leg to the rear, shifting the weight from the support leg onto the top of your foot. Keep the knee of the supporting leg turned out to reduce risk of injury. The torso twists, lowering the chest over the knee of the supporting leg. Both arms reach to the floor to catch the body on the "fall." With the weight distributed over your arms, slide the supporting leg along the floor to meet the sliding leg. Push your body sideward along the floor by extending your arms to end in a side-lying position (Figure 8-17).

The Slide to Prone Fall

Perform the slide to prone fall as described above in the sideward fall. At the moment when the "fall" occurs and the weight of your body is held by your arms, rotate your body to a front fall position as the supporting leg slides toe under to meet the sliding leg. Push your body to a prone position along the floor by extending your arms. Keep your body tight by contracting the abdominal and gluteal muscles. End in a prone lying position (Figure 8-18).

FIGURE 8-16 The backward fall

FIGURE 8-17 The sideward fall

FIGURE 8-18 The slide to prone fall

Chorus Line

CHAPTER 9
PUTTING IT ALL TOGETHER

Dance not only is composed of dance steps but also includes the elements of time, space, and dynamics. By understanding these elements, the dancer can create exciting movements without having years of dance training. The variation of time, space, and dynamics gives life to the dance and energy and enthusiasm to the dancer. The dancer's ability to manipulate these elements is essential for an exciting performance. This chapter discusses these elements of dance and also demonstrates how to turn dance movements into an artistic expression through the use of projection. The concept of performance and dance as a creative expression is especially highlighted in the discussion on projection, improvisation, and the ultimate craft of choreography.

TIME: FIND THE BEAT AND COUNT IT

As colors create a mood in painting, music sets the mood in dance. Music is very often the inspiration for the dance. Choreography can be seen as a response to the mood and tone set forth by the musical phrases. When there is an accent in the musical phrase, the movement will often emulate that accent. Most important, the rhythmic structure underlying all dance movements is also provided by the music.

Because of the relationship between dance and music, it is essential that the dancer has an understanding of music and is able to count the beat, recognize the accents, and hear the rhythmic patterns and musical phrasing. Let's begin by analyzing the structure of music.

Beat

The **beat** is the basic unit of musical time. The beat can be heard as a regular pulsation underlying the music; it is similar to the ticking of a clock.

Tempo

The **tempo** of a piece of music is the speed at which it is performed. A number of Italian terms are used to indicate the tempo of a piece. Listed from the slowest to the fastest, they are

Largo	Very slow, broad	*Allegretto*	Fast
Lento	Slow	*Allegro*	Fast ("cheerful")
Adagio	Slow ("at ease")	*Presto*	Very fast
Andante	Moderate ("walking")	*Prestissimo*	As fast as possible
Moderato	Moderate		

Meter and Measure

Written music is divided into groups of notes called **measures** (also known as **bars**), each having a specific number of beats. **Meter** is the basic number of beats per measure.

Time Signature

The meter of a piece of music is indicated by a **time signature** at the beginning of the piece. The time signature is written as two numbers. The first number indicates the number of beats per measure; the second number indicates the kind of note (half note, quarter note, etc.) that receives one beat. The common waltz time signature, 3/4, indicates that there are three beats to the measure and that a quarter note receives one beat.

Note Values

Written music shows not only which note should be played, but the relative duration of one note to another through a system of **note values**. At the top of the note-value tree shown in Figure 9-1 is a whole note. Each of the lines below it is equal in duration to a whole note. Two half notes equal a whole note, as do four quarter notes, eight eighth notes, and sixteen sixteenth notes. It should be understood that these note values are relative to each other, rather than absolute, since the time allotted the notes depends on the tempo of the piece.

Simple Meter

Simple meters have two, three, or four beats per measure. Examples of simple meter are

2/2, 2/4, 2/8	Two beats per measure
3/2, 3/4, 3/8	Three beats per measure
4/2, 4/4, 4/8	Four beats per measure

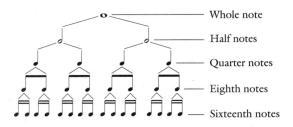

FIGURE 9-1 Note-value tree

In jazz music, simple meters are sometimes combined to form **irregular meters,** such as 5/4—a combination of the simple meters 2/4 and 3/4. Unusual meters such as 5/4 and 7/4 are frequently used by such jazz composers as Dave Brubeck and Bill Evans.

Compound Meter

Compound meters are simple meters multiplied by three. Examples of compound meter are

6/2, 6/4, 6/8	Six (3 × 2) beats per measure
9/4, 9/8	Nine (3 × 3) beats per measure
12/4, 12/8	Twelve (3 × 4) beats per measure

Mixed Meter

In **mixed meter,** the time signature may change several times within a single piece of music. Examples of mixed meter may be found in many Beatles' songs:

"Good Day Sunshine"	4/4, 3/4
"All You Need Is Love"	4/4, 3/4, 4/4, 3/4, 4/4, 2/4
"Strawberry Fields Forever"	4/4, 2/4, 4/4, 2/4, 6/8, 9/8, 4/4
"Blackbird"	3/4, 4/4, 6/4, 4/4, 6/4, 3/4

Accent and Syncopation

Accent is emphasis on one note or chord. In simple meter, the accent is generally on the **downbeat**—the first beat of the measure. **Syncopation** places the accent on normally unaccented beats of the measure. The three most common means of syncopation are (1) holding a note on the first beat for the length of two beats; (2) skipping the first beat altogether and replacing it with a silence (a **rest**); and (3) accenting normally weak beats, such as the **upbeat**—the last beat of the measure. Another means of syncopation common to jazz music is to create a hesitation by playing a note slightly sooner or later than it would normally be played. Syncopation, a trademark of jazz, adds to the surprise and spontaneity of jazz dance.

Rhythmic Pattern

Rhythmic pattern is created by the combination of note values, accents, and meter. For example:

A simple waltz in 3/4 time with the accent on the first beat of the measure would have a rhythmic pattern of **one**-two-three, **one**-two-three, **one**-two-three.

A typical march in 2/4 time with the accent on the first beat would have a rhythmic pattern of **one**-two, **one**-two, **one**-two.

Normally accented 4/4 time would have a rhythmic pattern of **one**-two-*three*-four, **one**-two-*three*-four, with the major accent on the first beat and a lesser accent on the third beat.

A syncopated rhythm in 4/4 time might have a rhythmic pattern of one-**and**-two-**and**-three-**and**-four-**and,** one-**and**-two-**and**-three-**and**-four-**and;** or, accenting the upbeat, one-two-three-**four,** one-two-three-**four,** one-two-three-**four.**

More-complicated rhythmic patterns are created as notes of differing values are combined (see Figure 9-2).

Musical Phrases

A **musical phrase** is a division of the musical line, somewhat comparable to a clause or a sentence in prose. Although it may take some practice for you to recognize musical phrases, it will be helpful to think of them as short musical statements that come to recognizable points of arrival—points where a singer might take a breath.

A musical phrase is at least two measures long. In jazz dance classes, music in 4/4 time is usually counted in two-measure phrases totaling eight counts. Breaking the sequence of a dance combination into phrases of eight counts makes it easier for the dancer to remember the steps. When counting and keeping track of the phrases, the teacher will very often number them by counting 1-2-3-4-5-6-7-8, 2-2-3-4-5-6-7-8, 3-2-3-4-5-6-7-8, etc.

An understanding of basic musical terms is essential to the beginning dancer. With continued exposure to music, a dancer will develop an ability to recognize tempos, meters, accents, rhythmic patterns, and musical phrases.

EXAMPLE 1

Beat (4/4 meter)	1	2	3	4
Musical notation				
Rhythmic pattern	1 &	2 &	3 &	4 &

EXAMPLE 1

Beat (4/4 meter)	1	2	3	4
Musical notation				
Rhythmic pattern	1 a &	2 &	3 a &	4

FIGURE 9-2 Complicated rhythmic patterns

Exercises for the Study of Time

Exercise 1 Using either a drum or recorded music, perform a simple movement, such as a jazz walk, across the floor. Move four counts on the beat: 1-2-3-4. Next, move four counts off the beat: 1-**and**-2-**and**-3-**and**-4-**and**. Alternate every four counts, first moving on the beat, then off the beat.

Exercise 2 Listen to music with 4/4 meter and identify its accent. Once the accent is identified, move only on the accented beats, holding the movement during the unaccented beats. Repeat this exercise with 2/4 and 3/4 meter.

Exercise 3 Perform a simple locomotor movement, such as a walk or run, for an entire musical phrase. When a new phrase begins, perform a new locomotor movement. Continue this exercise through an entire piece of music.

Exercise 4 Practice clapping the following rhythmic patterns and then choreograph movements that coincide with these patterns:

a. 1 & a 2   3 & 4   c. 1   2   3 & a 4 &
b. 1 &   2 & a 3   4 & a   d. 1 & a 2   & 3

SPACE

In addition to an awareness of the element of time—the **when** in dance: when to move, step, gesture, turn, and jump—the dancer must also develop a sensitivity to **space.**

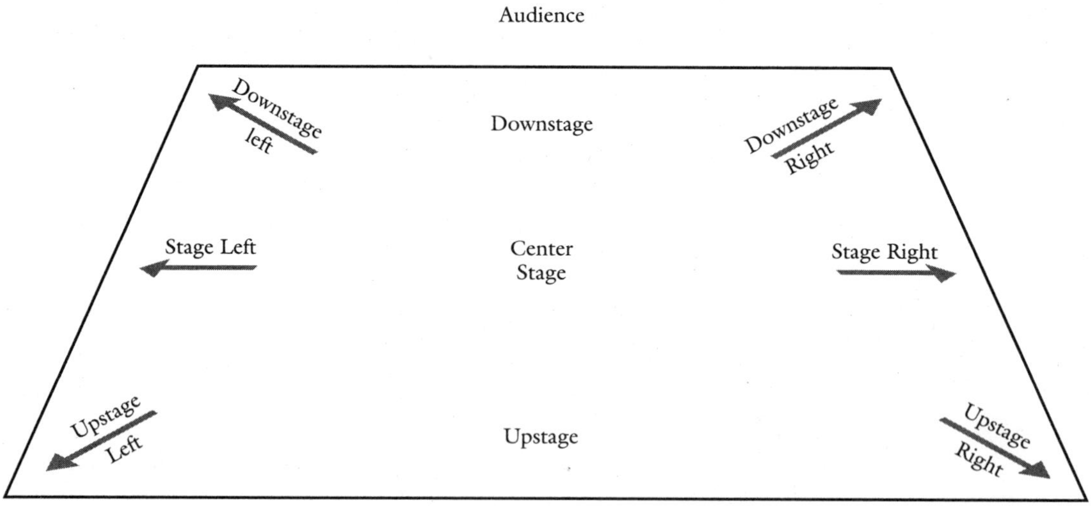

Audience

FIGURE 9-3 Stage directions

Awareness of space is the knowledge of **where:** where the dancer must go in relationship both to the other dancers in the space and to the audience. The dancer's space is affected by the direction the movement takes, the two-dimensional pattern created by the movement, the level of the movement, and its dimension or size.

Direction

Primary movement directions are forward, backward, sideward, diagonal, and circular. These directions can be expressed by conventional stage terminology (Figure 9-3). **Downstage** is the part of the stage closest to the audience. **Upstage** is the part of the stage farthest from the audience. **Stage left** is to the performer's left while facing the audience. **Stage right** is to the performer's right while facing the audience.

Floor Pattern

The **floor pattern** is the two-dimensional path a dancer follows. The floor pattern is affected by the dance steps and the dancer's position in relation to other dancers on the stage and to the audience. The more dancers onstage, the more intricate the patterns can become. Primary floor patterns are the square, circle, rectangle, triangle, zigzag, and figure eight (Figure 9-4).

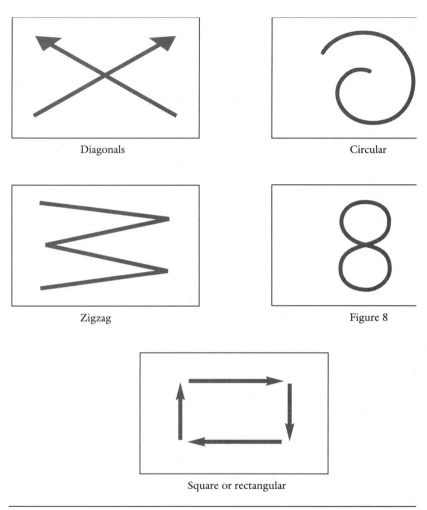

Diagonals

Circular

Zigzag

Figure 8

Square or rectangular

FIGURE 9-4 Floor patterns

Level

Level changes are determined by the positions the body assumes and by the height of the dancer in the space. Level changes create variety within the individual dancer's movements. Primary movement levels are lying, sitting, kneeling, standing, and jumping. Exciting level changes can occur with the use of varied jumps and falls.

Dimension

Dimension refers to the size of a dance movement and the space occupied by the body. The dimension of a movement can be altered in length, depth, or breadth. For example, a walk may be performed with big or small steps, thereby altering its length and affecting the amount of space the body occupies. The dimension of a movement is often affected by the other dancers occupying the space. When all dancers are performing the same movement, they must execute it with the same dimension or else they may find they have infringed on another's space.

Exercises for the Study of Space

Exercise 1: Direction   Select a locomotor movement. Perform the movement traveling in all the primary directions: forward, backward, sideward, diagonal, and circular.

Exercise 2: Spatial Pattern   Select a simple locomotor combination. Perform the combination in the primary spatial patterns: square, circle, rectangle, triangle, zigzag, and figure eight.

Exercise 3: Level   Perform a simple upper-body movement. Repeat it lying, sitting, kneeling, standing, and jumping.

Exercise 4: Dimension   Select a simple eight-count dance combination. Make the movements as large as possible; then make the movements as small as possible.

DYNAMICS

Dynamics refers to **how** a movement is performed: the intensity of its energy and the dynamic qualities of its performance. The same movement will appear different, depending on the intensity of the energy used for its performance. For example, raising an arm as if it were light as a feather would take minimal energy, whereas raising an arm as if it were a heavy log would take greater energy. Both the appearance and performance of these two moves would be different. It is the intensity of the energy output that creates the variety.

This section presents the terms commonly used to describe dynamic qualities in jazz dance. These qualities are affected by the intensity of the energy with which the movement is performed.

Percussive movement has a sharp, striking quality. There is a sharp, forceful initiation of movement and a definite cessation of movement. A percussive movement often appears as an accent because it is a sudden use of energy. This accent may be strong or slight, depending on the intensity of energy. A stomp, clap, snap, and punch are examples of accented or percussive movements.

Sustained movement has a prolonged quality and seems to have no beginning or end. Sustained movement is smooth, restrained, continuous, and unaccented. A slow, controlled lift of the arm is an example of a sustained movement.

Vibratory movement has a shaking or trembling quality. Vibratory movements may be very fast, recurring percussive movements, which in jazz dance may be performed by isolated body parts. A shoulder shimmy is an example of vibratory movement.

Suspension of a movement is the period of time during which the motion of a movement is lifted and held — the brief moment before the body succumbs to the pull of gravity. Suspended movement has a quality of weightlessness or breathlessness; it is often observed in a leap at the moment when the dancer appears suspended in air. It is also a hold in any movement before its completion.

A **swing** is akin to a pendulum movement. The speed of a swing increases at the bottom of its path and slows as the swing rises. Before the repetition of the pendulum swing, there seems to be a momentary pause, which has the quality of a release of body tension.

A **collapse** is the total release of body tension, the yielding to the pull of gravity. The collapse is often followed by a recovery movement.

Exercises for the Study of Dynamics

Exercise 1   Select a simple movement combination. Perform the combination three times, each time using a different energy level:

a.   As little energy as possible

b.   The maximum amount of energy

c.   A varied energy level

Exercise 2   Select a simple movement combination. Perform the combination six times, each time using a different dynamic quality:

a.	Percussive movement	d.	Suspension
b.	Sustained movement	e.	Swing
c.	Vibratory movement	f.	Collapse

PROJECTION

The concept of projection must also be explored before the dancer can fully appreciate the joy of dancing.

Projection is the communication of a vivid image to the audience through attitude, eye contact, facial expression, and full body commitment to the dance movements. A dancer who projects well is able to easily communicate the elements of time, space, and dynamics. In fact, without this full commitment to the dance, the artistic expression is lost within the dancer. By developing the ability to project, the dancer can strongly affect the audience and gain a sense of self-fulfillment from having given an emotionally moving performance.

To understand the importance of projection, observe professional performances and note that the dancers who catch your attention are those who not only have excellent technique but also extend the energy of the movements to every muscle in their faces and bodies. These performers have a distinct presence on stage.

For beginning students, the development of projection can be a creative and self-actualizing process. It is a challenge to perform the dance movements accurately and yet be free to expand one's focus beyond oneself. At all times the dancer should be continually aware of the importance of projection, whether it be to an audience, to other students in class, to the teacher, or only to the image in the mirror. The ability to project one's inner feelings comes with confidence in one's technical ability. When the confidence becomes habitual, the dancer's individual style becomes apparent and the performance becomes unique and truly exciting.

A good exercise to experience this complete immersion in the movements is to visualize an audience, perform a well-practiced combination, and attempt to project energy to the last row in the theater.

IMPROVISATION

The dictionary defines **improvisation** as "making something up on the spur of the moment." Professional musicians and dancers often improvise. Improvisation can also be useful and exciting for the beginning jazz dancer.

Sometimes just "letting loose" is valuable as a method for exploring undefined movement. Improvisation tends to be more valuable, however, if it is developed in response to a single idea, or theme. A visual image or musical phrase may be the stimulus for improvisation. Or, a dancer may take one movement or movement phrase and develop that by using the tools of time, space, and dynamics. Simple activities that can be used for motivating improvisation follow. Use the tools of dance — space, dynamics, and time — to create variety in the movements.

Exercise 1 Perform an eight-count sequence learned in class. Improvise two, four, six, or eight counts of your own to add to the sequence. Repeat the original combination.

Exercise 2 Take 16 counts to get to a position on the floor and then perform an eight-count sequence learned in class. Follow this with eight counts to return to a standing position.

Exercise 3 Take a step in any direction on the first count and clap on the second. Walk in one of the primary spatial patterns for eight counts. Take eight counts to stretch your body and end with an eight-count sequence.

Exercise 4 Walk or run anywhere in the room for eight counts. Change your level for eight counts and recover in eight counts. Incorporate a turning movement in an eight-count sequence. End with eight counts of a combination learned in class.

JAZZ DANCE CHOREOGRAPHY

Improvisation is the seed of creativity, and choreography is the development and growth of that seed. Once students are comfortable with improvisation, they should use it as a tool to help them choreograph combinations. Choreography is the setting of movements, unlike improvisation in which the moves are different every time they are performed. When a piece is choreographed, it is always the same; the movements are set.

In many jazz dance courses, the student is given the opportunity to choreograph a dance combination. Certain logical steps are usually followed when choreographing:

- Select the music.
- Analyze the music.
- Select movements that require improvising to the music.
- Create patterns of movement that coordinate to the size of the group that will be dancing.
- Develop dance movements that fit with the music and the mood.

Music Selection

The choreographer's first decision is to choose the music. It is vital that the music inspire movement. Listen and move to various music selections.

Music Analysis

Once the music is selected, listen to the piece many times. Count the measures in the music, using eight beats to the measure, since that is the most understandable count for dancers. After the measures are counted, group them into musical phrases. Finally, listen for phrases that are repeated in the music. Make notes on each phase of the musical analysis.

Movement Selection

After analyzing the music, attempt various dance movements with the phrases, trying to introduce jumps, turns, and floorwork in appropriate places. Through trial and error you will find movements that seem to coincide with the music.

Improvise a phrase of movement to a phrase of music. Create a new movement phrase when the musical phrase changes. Repeat movement phrases when the musical phrase repeats. Repetitive movement phrases build continuity and restate the theme of the dance. Create accents in dance movements to coincide with musical accents. Movement phrases that complement and contrast with a phrase of music may also be used to add new dimension to the music instead of merely reflecting it.

Make use of your total movement vocabulary. Do not hesitate to create new movements or to use movements performed by other dancers. You can create variation in dance movements by using all the elements of dance: time, space, and dynamics. Perform the movements in different tempos, in different directions, or with different dynamics.

Group Size Selection

In a solo dance performance, emphasis is placed on the technical and creative aspects of the dance movements. The audience's full attention is concentrated on the single dancer, so the dancer must perform with technical clarity and virtuosity. The solo performance is usually awarded to the most technically advanced dancer or one who exhibits a unique and exciting stage personality.

A group dance presents more possibilities in terms of floor pattern, spatial design, and movement interchange between dancers. As a result, fewer difficult dance movements are needed for a successful piece of dance choreography (see Figure 9-5). The possibilities for grouping dancers increase as the number of dancers increases.

In a group dance, all dancers need not be on the stage at the same time. Interesting floor patterns and spatial designs can be created with entrances and exits. Another means of creating interest is to vary the tempo, direction, or quality of a movement phrase as it is performed by different

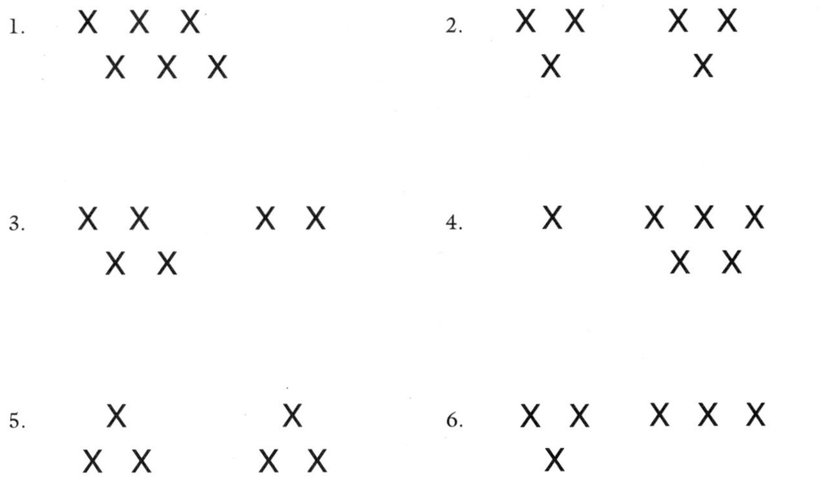

1.   X X X
         X X X

2.   X X   X X
         X   X

3.   X X   X X
         X X

4.   X   X X X
                     X X

5.   X   X
      X X   X X

6.   X X   X X X
         X

FIGURE 9-5 Spatial design possibilities when there are six dancers

subgroups. A group dance can also be diversified by solos, duets, trios, or quartets. A common choreography tool used in group dances is the canon. A **canon** is a round, such as "Three Blind Mice," in which the group is divided into subgroups that repeat and interact with one another. The effect of the canon is that each subgroup appears to be performing different movement phrases when, in fact, each subgroup is performing the same movement phrases, but at different times.

Dance Movement Development

Keep notes of your choreography so that you have a reference to the specific counts and movements. In particular, when working with groups, dancers may want choreography notes for personal practice. There are certain standard dance abbreviations that are commonly used when recording choreography. A list of these abbreviations is included in Table 9-1. Use these abbreviations to make notating your choreography an easier task.

During the student's initial attempts at choreography, it is beneficial to experiment with both solo and group choreography. Choreography is a valuable experience. It encourages creativity and discipline, thus promoting the overall development of the dance student.

TABLE 9-1 DANCE ABBREVIATIONS

R	right
L	left
1st	first position
2nd	second position
4th	fourth position
// 1st	parallel first position
X	cross (e.g., L X behind R = left cross behind right)
2X	crossed (e.g., fists 2X = with fists crossed)
X arms	crossed arms
"L" arm(s)	arm(s) lifted, bent at elbow
V arms	arms raised (elbows straight) to make V shape
= arms	arms parallel (across body or face)
DS	downstage
US	upstage
SR	stage right
SL	stage left
DSR	downstage right
DSL	downstage left
USR	upstage right
USL	upstage left
Dbl	double
pdb	*pas de bourrée*
kbc	kick-ball change

TABLE 9-1 DANCE ABBREVIATIONS (Continued)

T/O	turned out
R X L	right leg cross over left
L-R	left then right
R-L	right then left
4 hold	hold on count 4 (no movement)
ct, cts	count, counts
w/	with

Ann Reinking

CHAPTER 10

FITNESS FOR THE JAZZ DANCER

Jazz dance is a performing art. It is also physical exercise. When a student attends jazz dance classes, both of these subjects should be addressed. This chapter defines fitness and discusses the role jazz dance classes play in attaining fitness goals.

The term *fitness* is broadly used and often vaguely defined. Many people perceive health and fitness as one and the same, yet there is a definite distinction between the two concepts. **Health** reflects a person's state of being; it is typically viewed as the presence or absence of disease. **Fitness,** however, is the ability to do physical activity or to perform physical work.

Within the definition of fitness lie major components that are the foundation for implementing a sound fitness program. Those components are strength, flexibility, endurance, and body composition. The combination of these components leads to the achievement of fitness.

STRENGTH

Strength is the ability of a muscle or a group of muscles to exert a force against resistance. Maximal strength is when a group of muscles exerts a force against a resistance in one all-out effort. An example of such an action is one maximum lift in a weight-lifting exercise.

The body needs muscular strength for several reasons. First, strong muscles increase joint stability, which makes the joints less susceptible to injury. Second, improved muscle tone helps prevent common postural problems. For example, strong abdominal muscles can help alleviate postural problems associated with the back. Often, back problems occur because the strength in the spinal muscles is greater than that in the abdominal muscles. Muscular imbalance can contribute to postural deviations such as lordosis (swayback), kyphosis (exaggerated outward curvature of the thoracic spine), and scoliosis (crookedness of the thoracic spine).

Third, the body needs muscular strength because it contributes to agility, helps control the weight of the body in motion, and helps the body maneuver quickly. For muscular strength to be increased, the muscles must be contracted against a heavy resistance. As the muscles become stronger, the resistance applied must be increased if muscular strength is to continue to increase.

Strength Development

Most jazz dance classes develop strength through isometric, or static, contraction. In an **isometric contraction,** tension is developed in the muscle, but the muscle does not shorten and there is no joint movement. A simple example of an isometric contraction is tightening the abdominal muscles (holding the stomach in). In a dance class, a dancer continually contracts isometrically by maintaining correct alignment. In particular, balance exercises require isometric contraction. The dances must use a wide variety of muscle groups to achieve balance and to move through the exercises in a controlled manner.

Jazz dance classes also develop strength through isotonic training. In an **isotonic contraction** the muscle shortens and joint movement occurs. Push-ups, leg lifts, and *pliés* are examples of isotonic exercises. The resistance used is your own body weight.

# FLEXIBILITY

Although **flexibility** is generally associated with the elasticity of muscles, the total concept of flexibility is denoted by the range of motion of a certain joint and its corresponding muscle groups. Flexibility is influenced by the structure of the joint's bones and ligaments, the amount of bulk that surrounds the joint, and the elasticity of the muscles whose tendons cross the joint.

The range of motion of the body's various joints is defined as **joint mobility.** Joint mobility is measured by the amount of movement that exists where two joint surfaces articulate with each other. The greater the range of motion at the joint, the more the muscles can flex and extend. This range of motion, or joint mobility, is specific to each joint in the body. For example, your hip joint may be extremely flexible, whereas your shoulder joint may be inflexible.

The movement range of muscles and joints not used regularly throughout their full range of motion becomes limited. There are several reasons why good joint mobility and muscular elasticity should be maintained. Good joint mobility and muscular elasticity can increase resistance to muscular injury and soreness. However, too much flexibility in certain joints—such as the weight-bearing joints of the hips, knees, or ankles—may make a person susceptible to injury or hamper performance. Loose ligaments may allow a joint to twist abnormally, tearing the cartilage and other soft tissue. In general, it is advisable to achieve and maintain a "normal" amount of flexibility throughout the body—normal range varies with each individual.

To increase flexibility, the muscles must be stretched about 10 percent beyond their normal range of motion. As flexibility increases, the range of the stretch must also increase for flexibility to continue increasing.

Flexibility Development

Dance requires a tremendous amount of flexibility. During the warm-up section of class, the muscles are warmed and then put through a lengthy routine of stretching, or flexibility-enhancing exercises. The hip joint receives a great deal of attention during the stretching routine. Hip-joint flexibility aids the dancer in achieving high leg lifts. The Achilles tendon needs flexibility for high jumps and smooth landings. The back must be flexible, as well as the ankles and shoulder joint, so that the body can achieve a myriad of positions. Because flexibility is so essential to the dancer, every jazz class focuses on exercises to achieve it.

ENDURANCE

Endurance is the ability of a muscle or group of muscles to perform work (repeated muscular contractions) for a long time. With endurance, a muscle is able to resist fatigue when a movement is repeated over and over or when a muscle is held in a static contraction. There are two types of endurance: muscular and cardiorespiratory.

Muscular Endurance

Muscular endurance is the ability of skeletal muscles to work strenuously for progressively longer periods of time without fatigue. Muscular endurance is attained by applying resistance to the muscles, either by adding weight or by increasing repetitions. Note that muscle endurance is highly specific; it is attained only by the specific muscles exercised.

In jazz dance class, during the floor warm-up, muscular endurance can be developed in the abdominals through the repetition of sit-ups.

Push-ups develop triceps and pectoral muscles. (Sit-ups and push-ups are presented in Chapter 6.) The repetition of *pliés, relevés,* and *battements* (these movements are discussed in Chapter 4) increases the muscular endurance of the leg muscles.

Cardiorespiratory Endurance

Cardiorespiratory endurance is the ability of the cardiovascular system (heart and blood vessels) and the respiratory system (lungs and air passages) to function efficiently during sustained, vigorous activity. Such activity includes running, swimming, and cycling. To function efficiently, the cardiorespiratory system must be able to increase both the amount of oxygen-rich blood it delivers to the working muscles and the amount of carbon dioxide and waste products that it carries away. For cardiorespiratory endurance to be developed, a person must regularly engage in aerobic activities.

Cardiorespiratory endurance may or may not be developed in a jazz dance class; it depends on the teaching style of the instructor. If the teacher leads you through a continuous warm-up for a half hour or more and the warm-up is vigorous enough to maintain a heart rate of at least 130 to 170 beats per minute, then you are developing your cardiorespiratory endurance. This type of exercise is **aerobic exercise.** *Aerobic* means "with oxygen"—that is, you are able to provide oxygen to the working muscles so they are able to contract without accumulating fatiguing waste products. If in the warm-up you frequently stop for corrections and explanations or if your heart rate does not reach 130 beats per minute, then you are not significantly taxing your cardiorespiratory system; cardiorespiratory endurance will not improve. Aerobic exercise must be sustained for about 20 minutes for improvement to occur. The best exercises to achieve cardiorespiratory endurance are jogging, swimming, biking, and aerobic dance.

The dancer must also perform anaerobic exercise. **Anaerobic exercise** occurs when the body works at a very high intensity and cannot deliver enough oxygen to prevent the buildup of lactic acid. The lactic acid makes the muscles feel fatigued very quickly, so anaerobic exercise can be sustained for only short bursts of 1 to 2 minutes. By continually stressing the anaerobic response, the body can gradually increase its tolerance of lactic acid. As a result, with conditioning, the body can prolong anaerobic bursts of energy.

Jazz dance stresses the anaerobic response with across-the-floor locomotion: jumps, leaps, turns, and fast footwork. Combinations of these movements usually last for up to 2 minutes. Routine jazz dance combinations also provide anaerobic exercise and improve anaerobic metabolism.

Training Principles

To affect the components of fitness we have discussed so far—strength, flexibility, muscular endurance, and cardiorespiratory endurance—we must apply certain training principles to fitness conditioning. Adhering to the following training principles will help you to achieve the many benefits from participating in dance as an exercise program.

Training Effect

The term **training effect** refers to the physiological changes that occur in the body due to regular and proper participation in an exercise program. To achieve a training effect and experience the benefits of exercise (whether strength, flexibility, or endurance), the individual must apply the concepts of

- Threshold of training
- Specificity principle
- Overload principle
- Progression

Threshold of Training

In developing physical fitness, there is a "correct" amount of exercise that will produce effective conditioning results. The **threshold of training** is the minimum amount of exercise necessary to produce improvements in physical fitness.

Each component of fitness—strength, flexibility, and endurance—has its own threshold of training.

Specificity Principle

The **specificity principle** (specific adaptations to imposed demands—SAID—principle) is a unifying concept that applies to all areas of fitness. It means that the human body adapts specifically to the demands placed on it. For example, strength training induces specific strength adaptations but does not develop flexibility.

The specificity principle also applies to each body part. If the legs are exercised, fitness is built in the legs. If the arms are exercised, fitness is built in the arms. Finally, the specificity principle applies to certain activities—specificity of training. Specific exercise elicits specific adaptations, creating specific training effects. Training is most effective when it closely resembles the activity for which a person is training, using the specific muscles involved in the desired performance. For example, for an individual to improve the performance of the shot put, the person must perform both an exercise that overloads the arm muscles and a training motion that closely resembles the motion of the shot put. Whatever you are trying to achieve, you must train your body specifically for that outcome.

Overload Principle

Jazz dance can be a way to achieve fitness. But like any means of fitness, for improvement to occur the **overload principle** must be applied. This means elected parts of the body must be subjected to loads greater than those to which they are accustomed. The principle can be summed up in this simple rule: Do more today than you did yesterday, and do more tomorrow than you did today.

The overload principle affects the development of strength, flexibility, and endurance. For muscular strength to increase, muscles must work against a greater-than-normal load. For flexibility to increase, muscles must be stretched beyond their current length. For endurance to improve, muscles must be exposed to increasingly more sustained work. For cardiovascular endurance to improve, there must be an increased demand on the heart and lungs.

Basically, the overload principle may be applied to a fitness program in five ways:

- Increase the number of repetitions or distance of the exercise.
- Increase the duration of the exercise.
- Increase the speed of the exercise.
- Increase the intensity or resistance of the exercise.
- Decrease the rest intervals between exercises.

How can the overload principle be applied to a jazz dance class? Flexibility can be increased by increasing the distance and duration of a stretch. Strength can be increased by increasing the duration of balancing. Muscular endurance can be increased by increasing repetitions, and cardiovascular endurance can be increased by decreasing rest intervals. Do not risk permanent injury by attempting too much too soon, however. Work under the supervision of a competent teacher who understands your level of experience and fitness. Positive results will come only when the body is challenged gradually.

Progression

Progression goes hand in hand with overload. When overload is applied to the workout, it must be done progressively, or a little bit at a time. When overloading the duration of an aerobic workout, the principle of progression would add 3 to 5 minutes to the workout once the initial workout had reached a comfortable state. Applying progression to intensity and frequency works the same way; once the exercise has achieved a comfortable state, slightly increase the intensity or add another day to the workout regimen. Never go from 2 days to 5 days all at once or 20 minutes to 40 minutes in one workout. Although the progression principle may appear to be a rule of logic and common sense, it is sometimes overlooked. Failure to adhere to a sound principle of progression may result in unnecessary soreness and/or injury.

Knowing the fitness values and principles that apply to a jazz dance class can provide motivation for working hard, working safely, and setting goals. But dance goes beyond the demands of exercise. Dance is an art form that is mentally and emotionally challenging. For the jazz dancer, fitness is a worthwhile by-product of the pursuit of perfection.

Body Composition

A final component in determining fitness is **body composition.** All too often we judge ourselves on how we look rather than on an accurate assessment of our body's fat and lean weight composition. However, looks can be deceiving!

Body composition is generally assessed by somatotyping (that is, describing body type by visual inspection) and by determining body fat. The body can be changed in body fat content through aerobic exercise, toning, and diet. Unfortunately, we cannot change our body type, no matter how hard we try. You can rid yourself of any obsession to look thin by understanding the body composition principles. You can also stop using the scale to determine how fat you are. Leanness is what counts, **not** lightness.

Fat Weight

There are two forms of body fat: essential fat and nonessential, or storage, fat. **Essential fat** is stored in the bone marrow, in organs such as the heart, lungs, liver, spleen, kidneys, and intestines, and in the liquid-rich tissues of the spinal column and brain. **Storage fat** accumulates in adipose tissue, the fatty tissues that protect the various internal organs and that are found in the subcutaneous fat deposited beneath the skin. A certain amount of storage fat is necessary for maintaining health and good nutrition. Women and men need different amounts of essential storage fat.

In females, a part of essential fat includes what is termed **sex-specific** or **sex characteristic fat.** For instance, in the total mass of body fat, approximately 4 percent is attributed to breast fat tissue. The difference in body fat for females is also related to hormonal and childbearing functions. Among certain groups of female athletes with low levels of body fat, menstrual irregularities and cessation of menstruation have occurred. Generally, a healthy, adult female should have 25 percent or less body fat and a healthy, active male, 15 percent or less body fat.

Lean Body Weight

Lean body weight is the collective weight of the bones, muscles, ligaments and connective tissues, organs, and fluids. During adulthood, changes in lean body weight may occur primarily because the body's muscles are not receiving as much exercise. Although your life may be filled with activity, do not confuse that activity with exercise, which stresses the muscles. You need to exercise your muscles regularly to keep them lean and dense.

TECHNIQUES FOR WEIGHT ASSESSMENT

Skinfold Measurement

A calibrated precision instrument called a **skinfold caliper** is used to measure several predetermined sites on the body to determine the amount of body fat that lies just under the skin. The measurements we describe below — the Pollock, Schmidt, and Jackson method — are taken at three skinfold sites and provide a fat percentage based on a subject's age. These measurements are then computed by a formula to assess the amount of total body fat.

   Although this method is relatively simple as compared to hydrostatic weighing and the body composition analyzer, it is not as accurate because it gives an estimate of only body fat, not body mass. The accuracy rate is ± 5 to 10 percent of body fat. Because approximately 50 percent of total body fat lies just under the skin and the skinfold test is easy to administer, the method is widely used. It is also a useful comparative test: The original body fat measurements can be compared with new measurements taken at the same sites after months of training or exercising.

Bioelectric Impedance Analysis

In bioelectric impedance analysis, a mild electric impulse is sent throughout the body to measure body density, determining the percentages of fat and lean body mass. A computer program is used to combine the electrical measurements with the input of a person's data, including age, gender, height, and weight. Standard equations are preprogrammed into the computer software to print out an estimate of the subject's percentage of body fat.

Although this technique is easy to administer, results can be affected by dehydration or overhydration of the body, as well as by skin temperature. Predicted body fat results may be less accurate than skinfold measurement and hydrostatic weighing.

Ultrasound

An ultrasound machine sends high-frequency sound waves into the body, penetrating the skin and adipose tissue to reach the muscle. When the sound waves reach the muscle, an echo returns to the machine. The time the sound wave takes to travel back is converted by the ultrasound unit to predict a value of body fat.

Hydrostatic Weighing

Body composition can be assessed directly by a method called **hydrostatic weighing.** The hydrostatic, or underwater immersion, test is a very accurate method for determining body composition. A person is weighed under water to determine body density: The more bone and muscle the person has, the more easily the person sinks. Because fat floats, the more fat a person has, the less the person weighs under water.

Hydrostatic weighing is not as simple as it sounds and is usually unavailable to most people because it is expensive and involves sophisticated laboratory equipment. You may inquire about this technique at colleges and universities; many schools use it in their physical fitness education programs.

SUMMARY

Although jazz dance is viewed as a performing art and a means of creative expression, it is also an excellent way to achieve physical fitness. Consistent class participation will lead to improved dance skill and enhanced physical fitness. Some students may notice increased flexibility, whereas others may note changes in muscle tone. Regardless of specific individual improvements, dancers will agree that jazz dance is an exciting combination of physical, mental, and emotional exercise!

Joseph Holmes Dance Theater

CHAPTER 11

The Dancer's Instrument: Taking Care of It

Although dance is an art form, it is also a demanding physical activity. Dancers must know how to keep their bodies healthy. In this chapter, injury prevention and care, exercise as a means for stress reduction, and sound nutritional concepts are presented.

Injury Prevention

Dance is not without risk of injury. However, the risk of injury decreases dramatically when you take certain precautions and perform exercises with careful attention to proper technique.

Self-Assessment

The first phase of injury prevention involves self-assessment. Evaluate your readiness to begin a dance program. If you are not sure you have the strength and stamina, discuss your doubts with the dance instructor or your doctor. Ask for an exercise program that will help you build your strength slowly and safely.

Soreness Prevention

Soreness is the most common ailment of the beginning dancer. There are two different types of soreness. Acute soreness, or general soreness, occurs during or immediately after an exercise session and disappears in 3 to 4 hours. Acute soreness is thought to be caused by inadequate blood flow to the exercising muscles (ischemia). This condition causes the accumulation of lactic acid and potassium products, which cause soreness. When blood flow returns, the buildup is diffused and soreness diminishes.

The second type of soreness is **delayed muscle soreness,** which increases for 2 to 3 days following exercise and then diminishes until it disappears completely after 7 days. The four popular theories about the cause of delayed muscle soreness involve lactic acid accumulation, muscle spasms, torn muscle tissues, and damaged connective tissues.

You can prevent soreness by:

- Warming up properly
- Avoiding bouncing-type (ballistic) stretching
- Progressing slowly in the initial phases of class
- Cooling down properly with adequate stretching

Expect some soreness if you have been inactive before starting your dance class. Do not stop exercising merely because you are a little sore — the soreness will only recur later when you attempt another exercise program.

Warm-Up and Cool-Down as Means to Injury Prevention

To prevent injuries, do pre–warm-up exercises. (Pre–warm-up, or alignment, exercises are presented in Chapter 3. Warm-up exercises are discussed in Chapter 6.) Maintain proper form and technique in class. In addition, cool down before leaving the classroom.

The cool-down prepares the body for rest, just as the warm-up prepares the body for action. When you dance, the heart pumps a large amount of blood to the working muscles, to supply them with oxygen needed to keep moving. As long as dancing continues, the muscles squeeze the veins, forcing the blood back to the heart. When the class ends abruptly with an exciting combination or tricky locomotor phrase, the blood is left in the working muscles. In the case of the jazz dancer, the blood tends to pool in the lower extremities. Because the heart has less blood to pump, blood pressure may drop and this, in turn, may cause dizziness or lightheadedness. A gradual tapering off of activity — a cool-down — allows the muscles to send the "extra" blood back to the heart and brain. The cool-down also helps prevent muscle soreness.

Most jazz classes do not incorporate a cool-down as part of the format. Give yourself a cool-down of 5 to 10 minutes before leaving the studio. A cool-down can begin with simple walking movements to slow the heart rate. Then incorporate any stretching exercise described in the pre–warm-up and warm-up sections of this book. Avoid stretches that bring your head below your heart during the first 5 minutes of the cool-down — this position may cause blood to rush to the brain and cause dizziness. To prevent dizziness, perform exercises in a standing position until your body has substantially recovered from the dance activity. Once this has occurred, any of the stretches described will be beneficial.

SPECIAL CONSIDERATIONS

Special considerations as to **when** we exercise may also be a precaution for preventing injury or pain. Certain circumstances may need special attention or may have particular procedures or guidelines to follow to reduce injury risk. Review the following situations to determine if any might be applicable to you.

With Pain from a Previous Injury

If you are recovering from an injury, you should carefully monitor the intensity of the exercise during the rehabilitation period. Although you may feel slight discomfort as you renew your exercise program, you should not feel pain per se. If pain does occur, stop the exercise; give your body more time to heal. You may want to choose an alternative exercise that does not affect the injury.

With a Cold

This is a very individual situation. If you have a slight cold, exercise may help to relive some of the aches and pains and make you feel better. A severe cold, on the other hand, could leave you without adequate strength and energy required for medical recovery. If you decide to exercise, remember to check your heart rate and exercise at a moderate workout level. Fluids are extremely important. Juices high in vitamin C are good to drink before or after the workout. If you are uncomfortable during the workout, **stop!** Resume your exercise program when you are in better health.

During Your Menstrual Cycle

As a general rule, there is no problem exercising during menstruation. In fact, it can help to improve blood circulation, which may make you feel more energetic. If heavy cramping makes it very uncomfortable to move, however, rest is encouraged. In this case, it is advisable to see a physician to help you through the pain.

In the Heat

When you exercise in the heat, your body has a more difficult time dissipating the internal heat because the external environment does not supply any relief. Profuse sweating often results and with it, a large amount of water loss. This could result in dehydration and, more seriously, heat exhaustion or heat stroke. It is acceptable to exercise in the heat provided the following precautions are taken:

Decrease the intensity of exercise beyond 30 minutes.

Exercise in the early morning or late evening.

Drink plenty of fluids before, during, and after exercising.

Wear lightweight and well-ventilated clothing to expose as much skin as possible to aid in the evaporation of sweat.

In the Cold

Generally, exercising in the cold will pose few problems if you are prepared. Usually, in this environment the body will stay cool and refreshed, but chilling can occur quickly if the body surface is wet with sweat and the dilation of the blood vessels continues to bring body heat to the skin. Therefore, after exercise you need to retain body heat. The following guidelines will prevent problems when you exercise in a cold climate:

1. Wear several layers of clothing that can be removed and replaced as needed.

2. Allow for adequate ventilation of sweat. If evaporation of sweat does not occur, the wet garments will drain the body of heat during rest periods.

3. Drink plenty of fluids, just as in the heat. Urine production increases in the cold, making fluid replacement important.

INJURY CARE

If an injury does occur, you should be aware of the proper and immediate means of treatment. Some injuries may merely require self-treatment. However, some injuries may require first aid or, depending on severity, professional diagnosis and treatment. Table 11-1 lists common dance injuries.

Apply first aid as soon as you incur an injury. Immediate treatment quickens the healing process. A simple way to remember the first-aid treatment is to keep in mind the acronym RICE. The letters stand for

Rest

Ice

Compression

Elevation

TABLE 11-1 COMMON DANCE INJURIES

INJURY	SYMPTOMS	CAUSE	TREATMENT
Muscle cramp	Painful, spasmodic contraction usually felt in back of the leg and front of the thigh.	Fatigue, muscle tightness, fluid, salt, or potassium imbalance from profuse sweating.	Gently stretch or massage area. Drink water and take potassium.
Muscle strain	Muscle tenderness and possible swelling.	Sudden contraction of muscle and poor flexibility.	Ice immediately. See physician if it does not improve.
Shin splints	Pain on anterior aspect of lower leg. Possible swelling.	Jumping on hard surfaces, improper landing, muscle imbalance.	RICE
Plantar fascitis	Chronic pain and inflammation to the foot, especially the heel. Longitudinal arch may also feel pain.	Overuse by putting too much stress on foot.	RICE. See physician.
Ankle sprain	Swelling, inflammation, point tenderness, swelling.	Unstable landings, rolling over on ankle	Ice immediately. See physician.
Patellar tendinitis	Pain, tenderness, and inflammation below knee cap.	Repetitive jumping and landing activities.	RICE. See physician
Stress fracture	Chronic pain and swelling. Usually occurs in the shins or ball of foot.	Repetitive jumping and landing.	RICE. See physician.

RICE: The Recipe for First Aid

Rest   Stop using the injured area as soon as you experience pain.

Ice   Apply ice immediately to the injured area for 15 to 20 minutes several times a day for the first 48 hours after the injury has occurred. Ice reduces swelling and alleviates pain. Let the injured body part regain its normal body temperature between icings.

Compression   Firmly wrap the injured body part with an elastic or compression bandage between icings. A change in color or loss of normal sensation in the extremities indicates that the bandage is wrapped too tightly.

Elevation   Raise the injured part above heart level to decrease the blood supply to the injured area.

Self-Care Injuries

The following injuries do not usually require a trip to the doctor. If an injury does not heal with home care, however, consult a physician.

Blisters   A blister, caused by friction, is an escape of tissue fluid from beneath the skin's surface. You should not pop or drain a blister unless it interferes with your daily activity to the point where it absolutely has to be drained. If the blister has to be drained, clean the affected area with antiseptic. Then lance the blister with a sterile needle at several points. Forcibly drain the blister. As the area dries, leave the skin on for protection until it forms new skin; then clip away the dead skin. You can prevent most blisters by taking sensible care of your feet and wearing properly fitting footwear.

Cramps   A cramp is a painful spasmodic muscle contraction lasting anywhere from a few seconds to several hours. Muscle cramps commonly occur in the back of the lower leg (calf), the back of the upper leg (hamstring muscle group), and the front of the upper leg (quadriceps muscle group). Cramps are related to fatigue; muscle tightness; or fluid, salt, and potassium imbalance. To relieve the pain, gently stretch and/or massage the cramped muscle area. Since muscle cramps can be caused by a fluid and mineral imbalance from profuse sweating, drink water freely and increase your potassium intake naturally with foods such as tomatoes, bananas, and orange juice.

Muscle Strains   One type of muscle strain is the muscle pull, or damage to the muscle tissue. Scar tissue forms in the damaged area, and—because scar tissue is not as resilient as muscle tissue—you feel the effect of the pull for a long time. Another type of muscle strain involves the tissue around the muscle. The tendons, for example—the tissues that attach muscles to bones—often sustain strains. The blood supply to muscle-surrounding tissues is smaller than to the muscles; therefore, strains in these tissues take longer to heal than muscle pulls.

If you strain a muscle, apply ice as an immediate first-aid treatment. Rest the injured area. Healing is affected by many factors—age, physical condition, and so on—so citing an "average" healing time could be misleading. If the condition of your strain does not improve in what you consider a reasonable time for you, consult a doctor.

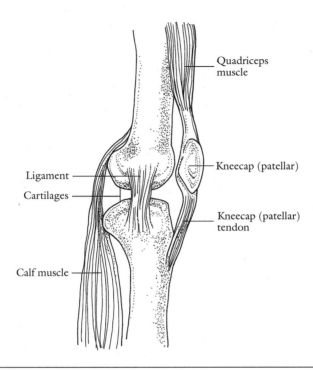

Quadriceps muscle

Ligament

Cartilages

Calf muscle

Kneecap (patellar)

Kneecap (patellar) tendon

FIGURE 11-1 Structures of the knee joint

Injuries Needing Professional Attention

Dancers are susceptible to several injuries that warrant professional medical attention: patellar tendinitis, shin splints, and sprains.

Patellar Tendinitis   Repetitive jumping and landing can produce small scars in the patellar tendon (Figure 11-1), causing pain, tenderness, and inflammation directly below the kneecap. This condition is **patellar tendinitis,** also called jumper's knee. Often, the aching of the knees apparent at the beginning of a workout disappears after warm-up. However, pain recurs when activity ceases. In a worsened condition, pain continues throughout a workout, and pressing on the tendon itself causes pain.

Shin Splints   Pains in the front of the lower leg are called **shin splints.** Shin splints indicate overuse or improper use of the muscles around the shin bone. The most frequent causes are shoes that give insufficient support, fallen arches, lack of conditioning, and the impact from landings on a hard surface.

Shin splints are common ailments, especially among beginning dancers. If your pain continues after first-aid treatment, however, see a doctor. Shin splints can develop into stress fractures.

To prevent shin splints, do a thorough warm-up, paying special attention to the calf muscles and ankles. If necessary, strengthen the shin muscles by performing appropriate exercises. Learn to use the *pliÇ* to absorb the shock of landing from jumps, leaps, and hops. Land on the ball of the foot, rolling the foot until the heel comes in contact with the floor.

Sprains   More serious than a strain, a sprain is a sudden or violent twisting of a joint, causing the ligaments to stretch or tear. The blood vessels often rupture, causing hemorrhage in the surrounding tissues. Symptoms of a sprain are swelling, inflammation, joint tenderness, and discoloration. Ankle sprains are common because the ligaments on the outside of the ankle joint are the weakest in the ankle. Therefore, the ankle is susceptible to injury incurred by rolling over on the outside of the foot.

Take precautions and use common sense in your dance training. If you are injured, remember the simple steps of first-aid treatment: rest, ice, compression, and elevation. Apply the treatment immediately after injury occurs. Seek medical advice for injuries that persist or are serious.

Exercise as a Means to Control Stress

Exercise can be a tool for releasing daily tension and increasing your ability to understand stressful conditions. Although experts cannot agree about exactly how exercise works this way, various theories suggest (1) that exercise may simply be a diversion, freeing the mind from stresses that contribute to anxiety; (2) that a feeling of accomplishment (of a physical goal) is a factor; and (3) that exercise reduces muscular tension, thus inducing a state of muscular relaxation. If you exercise to help reduce stress, you must not overexercise, which will re-create a state of stress.

Nutrition for Dancers

Because dance is such a physically demanding activity, dancers must develop an acute awareness of how to care for their bodies in all ways. One of the most overlooked means of caring for our bodies is our nutritional habits. Dancers must be especially aware of nutritional needs because of the intense demands dance places on the body. Dance requires strength and endurance, which the body cannot produce if it is not properly fueled. The body's fuel is food, the source of energy to maintain life and perform work.

TABLE 11-2 CALORIC VALUES OF NUTRIENTS

NUTRIENT	CALORIC VALUE
Protein	4 kilocalories per gram
Carbohydrate	4 kilocalories per gram
Fat	9 kilocalories per gram
Alcohol	7 kilocalories per gram

Calories

The energy food releases is measured in **calories,** or more specifically, **kilocalories.** The number of calories the body needs varies widely among individuals.

Virtually all the calories of energy the body uses are supplied by carbohydrates, fats, and proteins. Carbohydrates are the body's primary energy source. Fats are used if the carbohydrate supply is too low to meet the body's basic energy needs. Proteins provide an alternate energy source; the body uses them only when there are not enough calories available in the form of carbohydrates and fats. Protein is rarely used as an energy source; its most important function is to aid the body's growth and repair.

The amount of calories the body requires depends on the amount of calories (energy) it expends.

The energy output to maintain life functions—respiration, digestion, circulation, and nerve, hormonal, and cellular activities—is called the **basal metabolic rate (BMR).** This is approximately two-thirds of a person's energy use each day. Other energy output is for physical activities. The amount of energy you need each day depends on several factors, including, your age, size, and activity level. Energy is measured in calories, the fuel source for the body, and each and every food source has its own caloric value.

Not all foods are of equal caloric value. One food of equal weight to another can contain more calories just because of its value. Table 11-2 is a caloric value chart.

The type and combination of food fuel for the body is extremely important. We should all eat a well-balanced diet.

The Basic Four Food Group Plan has been modified to provide a better foundation for making food choices for a nutritionally adequate diet. The *Modified Basic Four Food Group Guide* includes food from the following categories:

1. Milk and milk products
2. Protein foods
    Animal sources
    Legumes
    Nuts
3. Fruits and vegetables
    Vitamin C–rich
    Dark green
    Other
4. Whole-grain cereal products
5. Fats and oils

In 1992, the U.S. Department of Agriculture developed a plan called the **Food Guide Pyramid.** In the Food Guide Pyramid, fruits and vegetables each have their own group. Fats, oils, and sweets are not considered a food group and are to be used sparingly. This pyramid and the recommended servings of each food group are shown in Figure 11-2. Either the Modified Basic Four Food Group Plan or the Food Guide Pyramid can provide a guideline for nutritionally sound food selection.

Nutrients

The food we eat is made up of nutrients. To fully understand the basics of proper nutrition, you should also become familiar with the types of nutrients that the body requires and their functions.

Protein   Protein is the basic structural substance of each cell in the body, and the main function of protein is to build and repair body tissue. Protein is also required to make hemoglobin, which carries oxygen to the cells. Protein is essential for muscular contraction during activity and plays an important role in regulating body fluids in acid base quality during vigorous exercise. Protein is also required to form antibodies in the bloodstream to fight off infection and disease.

Protein is made of basic building blocks called amino acids. Of the 22 amino acids in protein, 8 are considered essential. These essential amino acids cannot be manufactured in the body and therefore must be supplied through the food we eat. The protein in animal food sources is called complete because it contains the eight essential amino acids. The animal food sources are meat, fish, poultry, eggs, milk, and milk products.

Plant protein sources cannot supply the necessary total protein source because they lack one or more of the essential amino acids. However, when properly combined, these incomplete plant protein sources can provide all eight essential amino acids. Plant protein food sources are lentils, legumes, nuts, cereal, and tofu or other soybean products.

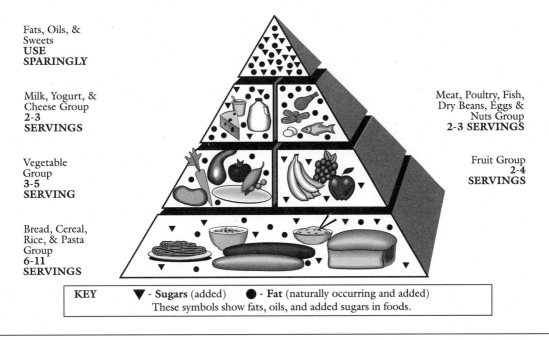

Fats, Oils, &
Sweets
**USE
SPARINGLY**

Milk, Yogurt, &
Cheese Group
**2-3
SERVINGS**

Vegetable
Group
**3-5
SERVING**

Bread, Cereal,
Rice, & Pasta
Group
**6-11
SERVINGS**

Meat, Poultry, Fish,
Dry Beans, Eggs &
Nuts Group
2-3 SERVINGS

Fruit Group
**2-4
SERVINGS**

KEY   ▼ - **Sugars** (added)   ● - **Fat** (naturally occurring and added)
These symbols show fats, oils, and added sugars in foods.

FIGURE 11-2 Food guide pyramid

To create complete proteins, combine animal proteins with grains or legumes, or combine different plant protein sources:

Animal Protein and Grains

- milk and cereal
- cheese pizza
- cheese and noodle casserole

Animal Protein and Legumes

- lentil soup and cheese toast
- chili with beans
- refried beans and cheese burrito

Plant and Plant Proteins

- beans and corn
- beans and rice
- beans and noodles
- black-eyed peas and rice

Tofu, a high-quality alternative to animal protein, is made from soymilk and is low in saturated fat and calories and free of cholesterol.

Protein intake should constitute approximately 12 percent of daily total calories. This means 6 to 9 ounces of protein per day or 0.9 gram of protein per kilogram of body weight (multiply your body weight in pounds by 0.424 to obtain your weight in kilograms). Pregnant and nursing mothers are exceptions to this protein requirement; they should increase their protein intake by 10 and 20 grams, respectively.

Many Americans eat an excess of protein, primarily animal protein. Although animal protein in a diet is a good way to ensure a balanced supply of essential amino acids, animal protein is high in saturated fats. Additionally, an excessive intake of protein can be stressful to the body in the process of breaking the protein down for fuel usage and for elimination. Most nutritionists recommend reducing the consumption of animal protein and increasing the intake of plant (vegetable) protein.

Fats   Dietary fats have the highest energy content of all nutrients. Fat's main function is to supply fuel and energy to the body, both at rest and during exercise. Fat also helps the body use the fat-soluble vitamins A, D, E, and K. Body fat also has other functions, such as providing cushioning for the body's vital organs and protection from extreme temperatures of cold.

Although there is no specific requirement for fat in the diet, there is a need for essential fatty acid and the vitamins that are the components of fat. Currently, about 40 percent of Americans' daily caloric intake is composed of fat. A recommended dietary goal is less than 30 percent, with the amount of saturated fat in the diet less than 10 percent. In general, to maintain a healthy diet, the total amount of fats in the diet should be reduced and saturated fats should be replaced with unsaturated fats.

When we are referring to fats we are really talking about **lipids.** The three lipids we are concerned with are triglycerides (fats and oils), phospholipids, and sterols.

Triglycerides   Triglycerides make up approximately 98 percent of our fat intake from food. All foods with fat contain a combination of saturated and unsaturated fats.

Saturated fats are found predominantly in animal meat, poultry fats, and animal products such as eggs and dairy items. Plant-saturated fats are found in coconut and palm oil, vegetable shortening, and commercial bakery pastries and sweets.

Unsaturated fats generally come from plant sources and are usually liquid at room temperature. Examples of monosaturated fats are canola, olive, and peanut oil. Unsaturated fats include safflower, sunflower, soybean, and corn oil.

Phospholipids   Phospholipids are important for blood clotting and are found in the structure of the insulation sheath of the nerve fibers. In the phospholipid family are lipoproteins, which transport fat in the blood. There are two types of lipoproteins: high-density lipoproteins and low-density lipoproteins.

Low-density lipoproteins (LDLs) have the least amount of protein and the greatest amount of fat. LDLs have the greatest amount of **cholesterol,** which is the fat in the blood and in tissues. Cholesterol is important to the production of hormones and enzymes, but when carried by the LDL, it tends to deposit on the arterial wall. The continued buildup of cholesterol narrows the artery, increasing the chances of coronary heart disease.

High-density lipoproteins (HDLs) have the greatest amount of protein and the least amount of fat and cholesterol. HDLs protect against heart disease. They compete with the LDLs to enter into the cells of artery walls. HDLs carry cholesterol deposited on the artery wall to the liver and then to the intestines to be excreted, thus combating the risk of coronary heart disease.

When a physician determines your cholesterol level, the amount of LDLs and HDLs can be determined and the ratio of these lipoproteins can help provide information in predicting the risk of coronary heart disease. The good news for people involved in a fitness program is that studies have shown that the HDL level can be increased with regular aerobic exercise.

Sterols The most widely known sterol is cholesterol. Cholesterol is found only in animal tissue that contains no fatty acids. Cholesterol is important in the production of hormones and enzymes and is also a part of cell membranes. Dietary cholesterol, which is the cholesterol found in animal products, raises the total level of blood cholesterol. When an excess of cholesterol is taken in the diet, it is deposited by the LDLs on the arterial walls. The highest amounts of cholesterol are found in liver and other organ meats and in egg yolks. To create a healthy diet and to lower the risk of coronary heart disease, dietary cholesterol should be reduced.

Carbohydrates Carbohydrates supply the body with its primary source of energy, glucose. Glucose (blood sugar) is the product of the digestion of carbohydrates and is stored in the muscles. Carbohydrates also provide fuel for the central nervous system and are a metabolic primer for fat metabolism.

Although all carbohydrates have a certain chemistry in common, there is a big difference between one carbohydrate and another. The two general types of carbohydrates are simple and complex. **Simple carbohydrates**—sugars—are maltose, which is found in malt; lactose, found in milk; and sucrose, which is table sugar. When these sugars are ingested, they are converted to blood glucose almost immediately. Therefore, the consumption of simple carbohydrates causes blood glucose levels to fluctuate too quickly, making energy levels vacillate. Table sugar and the refined and processed sugars found in sodas, candy, cookies, cakes, and a realm of other sweetened treats offer no nutrients, are high in calories, and are associated with tooth decay, obesity, malnutrition, diabetes, and hypoglycemia (low blood sugar).

Complex carbohydrates—starches—are the natural sugars found in fruits, vegetables, and grains. They are the best source of energy because they convert blood glucose slowly. In other words, they supply a sustained energy output.

Complex carbohydrates are probably the best foods we can eat because they are high in vitamins, minerals, and fiber. Fiber is the structural part of fruits, vegetables, legumes, cereals, and grains that humans cannot break down in the digestive system. It provides the roughage and bulk to keep the gastrointestinal tract working properly. Fiber has been shown to lower cholesterol and help control diabetes, and it may also help prevent colon cancer.

Daily caloric intake should include about 60 percent carbohydrates, with about half of that intake being complex carbohydrates. You should make every effort to decrease your intake of simple, "sugary" carbohydrates, which have no nutritional value, and increase your intake of complex carbohydrates, which offer vitamins, minerals, and fiber.

Water   Water is second to oxygen as a substance necessary to sustain life. An adequate supply of water is necessary for all energy production in the body, for temperature control (especially during vigorous exercise), and for the elimination of waste products. **Dehydration,** or the loss of water in the body, can increase the risk of heat exhaustion and heatstroke. You should include water as an essential part of your diet and be sure to drink water, especially before and after exercise.

Although a number of commercial products on the market are supposed to replenish the body by replacing not only fluids but also electrolytes and carbohydrates, these drinks contain sugar. Sugar slows the rate at which water leaves the stomach, thus delaying the rehydration process. The best way to replace fluid lost in exercise is with water; and cold water will leave the stomach more quickly than warm water, thus helping you cool down more rapidly.

Drinking six to eight glasses of water a day is recommended for health maintenance. If you are physically active, you need to drink more.

Alcohol   Alcohol remains the most widely used drug on American college campuses and is a major problem even in high schools. Although alcohol is a drug, it is classified as a nutrient because it provides energy; 1 gram of alcohol is equal to 7 kilocalories. Although it is classified as a nutrient, it adds no nutritional value to our diet. Alcohol is metabolized as a carbohydrate, is stored mainly as a fat, and has adverse effects on athletic performance. The use of alcohol decreases aerobic capacity and strength. Alcohol decreases the liver's output of glucose, a prime ingredient for the production of adenosine triphosphate (ATP). The use of alcohol increases fatigue, promotes difficulty in regulating body temperature, and dehydrates the body. Research published in the *Journal of the American Medical Association* (1994) notes that the consumption of one or two drinks a day has been associated with lowered heart attack mortality. However, consumption of three or more drinks a day has been linked to increased mortality from other causes. The general message is that alcohol consumption in excess may pose problems of fat accumulation and decrease in health.

Vitamins and Minerals   Vitamins help use and absorb other nutrients and are necessary for the body's normal metabolic functioning. Vitamins are classified as fat soluble or water soluble. **Fat-soluble vitamins** (A, D, E, and K) tend to remain stored in the body and are usually not excreted in the urine. An excess accumulation of these vitamins may be toxic to the body. **Water-soluble vitamins** (C and B complex) are excreted in the urine and are not stored in the body in appreciable amounts.

Minerals are the building materials for body tissues and serve as nerve regulators. Minerals, except iron, are excreted by the body after they have carried out the function they provide for the body. Because minerals are excreted, it is important to replace mineral losses regularly.

Vitamins and minerals work together to regulate body processes, releasing energy from food and helping to metabolize carbohydrates and fats. Although there is a growing concern regarding vitamin deficiency, most people, except for unusual cases, can easily obtain the required amount of vitamins and minerals through good nutritional habits. Table 11-3 provides a list of the major vitamins and minerals, their functions, and food sources.

WEIGHT LOSS: THE "SET POINT" THEORY

If weight loss were merely a reflection of decreasing total caloric intake by diet, it would be a simple matter to lose weight. Although weight loss normally occurs at the onset of a diet, the body's weight tends to stabilize at some new, lower level. To continue to lose weight becomes difficult. Long-term weight control is explained by new insights of weight control in the "set point" theory.

The set point theory maintains that the brain's hypothalamus regulates weight by comparing the body's current level of fat with a kind of constant internal standard. When a person's fat level falls below this internal standard, the body responds with increased appetite. If food intake is not increased, the body adjusts its metabolic rate to protect its usual level of fat stores. During a diet, when food intake is not increased to

TABLE 11-3 VITAMIN AND MINERAL FUNCTIONS AND FOOD SOURCES

VITAMIN	FUNCTION	SOURCE
A	Enhances quality of skin, clear vision; helps maintain strong teeth.	Fortified milk, carrots, pumpkins, sweet potatoes, squash, green vegetables.
B complex Folic acid	Prevents anemia, certain birth defects of the spine and brain; helps make DNA. Works best when combined with B12. Oral contraceptives may increase need for folic acid.	Dark green and leafy vegetables, enriched cereals, and legumes.
B6 pyrodoxine	For energy production and blood cell formation.	Avocados, baked potatoes, leafy green vegetables.
B12 cobalamin	Maintains red blood cells and functions of the nervous system. If B12 is low, aerobic capacity seems to diminish and you may experience difficulty with balance and coordination. Stress and medications can impair absorption. Vegetarians who do not eat meat, eggs, or dairy products can be at risk for B12 deficiency.	Raw oysters, raw clams, sardines canned in soybean oil, fish, liverwurst, creamed cottage cheese, milk, and eggs.
C	Helps make O_2-carrying red blood cells and hemoglobin, which are important for bones and teeth.	Citrus fruits, tomatoes, strawberries, green and red peppers, potatoes, cranberries, pineapple and orange juices.
D	Promotes bone growth and strength.	Fortified milk, egg yolk, tuna, salmon, cod liver oil, and liver. Liver intake should be monitored because of high cholesterol level.
E	For red blood cell formation.	Fortified cereals, nuts, seeds, and oils. Avocado, mango, spinach, sweet potato, wild rice.

meet the body's increased appetite demands, the body adjusts its metabolic rate by burning calories more slowly. When a dieter resumes normal eating patterns, it is not uncommon to experience weight regain due to the body's slower metabolic rate.

The body's slower metabolic rate also affects the total fat-burning capacity of the body. The slowdown of the body's fat-burning capacity is due partly to a decrease in lean body mass, or muscle. During dieting,

TABLE 1-3 VITAMIN AND MINERAL FUNCTIONS . . . (Continued)

MINERAL	FUNCTION	SOURCE
K	For bone metabolism and blood clotting. Reduces risk and severity of bone fractures. K in combination with calcium, magnesium, and boron is called the "bone formula."	Leafy green vegetables, cabbage, peas, cauliflower, kale, broccoli, watercress, and dried beans.
Calcium	Strengthens bones and teeth; essential for cell function, muscle contraction, blood clotting, and transmission of nerve impulses.	Dairy products, broccoli, salmon, sardines, tofu, kale, spinach, almonds.
Iron	Formation of hemoglobin and myoglobin, which aids in the storage transport of oxygen within cells. Is depleted with exercise due to sweating. Diets low in iron may lead to anemia.	Organ meats, egg yolk, fish, oysters, dried fruits, whole-grain cereals, and milk, legumes, apricots, greens, broccoli, molasses.
Magnesium	Facilitates intestine absorption of calcium; required for teeth and bone formation, muscle contraction, transmission of nerve impulses.	Chocolate, instant coffee, cashews, artichokes.
Potassium	In combination with sodium and calcium, it maintains normal heart rhythm, regulates body's water balance, aids in muscle contraction, and conducts nerve impulses.	Potatoes, legumes, citrus fruits, bananas, tomatoes, and leafy vegetables.
Zinc	Aids in wound healing and promotes mental alertness; necessary for stress and tissue repair. Intense exercise can decrease the body's zinc stores due to sweating.	Oysters, legumes, brewer's yeast, meat, whole-grain cereals, cashews, sunflower and pumpkin seeds, tofu.

much of the weight loss occurs from the fat that is burned in muscle tissue. Finally, dieting causes enzyme changes in the adipose tissue lipoprotein lipase (a fat-storing enzyme). When caloric intake is decreased, this enzyme is dramatically increased, causing the body to become more efficient at storing fat.

The set point theory maintains that to lose weight, the body's set point must be lowered. The most effective way to lower the set point is through exercise. Once the set point is lowered, the body will work to maintain the lower fat level, just as it tried to maintain the higher fat level described in the dieting process. As opposed to dieting, weight loss through exercise maintains muscle mass. Remember that most fat is burned within the muscle. Through exercise, fat is lost; thus the ratio of muscle to fat is increased. The increased ratio of muscle to fat also has long-term benefits, since muscle requires more calories than fat to maintain itself.

With respect to the set point theory, the type of exercise for weight control is crucial. Aerobic exercise is the most beneficial because it allows the body to burn fat effectively during exercise. To achieve weight loss, aerobic exercise must be done at a moderate pace and at least 5 days a week.

WEIGHT LOSS FALLACIES

Weight loss programs are promoted by every avenue of media possible. Promises of simple and easy methods of weight loss and body toning are weekly features. Avoid fad diets, many of which can produce hazardous health problems. Never eliminate calories totally from one food group, as is called for in many fad diets. If you lose weight quickly, your body does not have enough time to adapt to the lower calorie intake, so you usually gain back the lost weight. And diets that promote quick weight loss by the elimination of water cause dehydration and the loss of important minerals.

Avoid being fooled by products that produce weight loss through dehydration such as plastic/rubber garments, body wraps, or saunas and steambaths. It is extremely important to avoid weight loss programs that use diet pills that are addictive and may cause health problems such as increased blood pressure, irregular heartbeat, and insomnia. The effect of a suppressed appetite from the use of diet pills is temporary, as the body builds up a tolerance to these stimulants.

Other beauty claims of weight loss include spot reduction, or the removal of fat from one area. Fat can only be eliminated proportionally as a result of overall weight loss. For most women, by virtue of heredity or female hormones, the thighs and abdomen carry a protective layer of fat. These areas seem to be the first where fat appears and the last for fat to disappear during any change in body weight.

EATING DISORDERS

Anorexia nervosa is an eating disorder that involves severe food restriction as a means to weight loss. People who suffer from this disorder are usually very preoccupied with thinness and body image. They often include individuals involved seriously in an activity such as modeling or in a sport such as gymnastics or ballet that requires low body weight. A person suffering from anorexia may be recognized by a severe loss of weight. Anorexia may cause other health problems, such as retarded bone growth, anemia, low blood pressure, amenorrhea, low body temperature, low basal metabolism, slow heart rate, and other physiological body changes. Anorexia should be treated by a qualified professional.

Bulimia is an eating disorder that involves episodes of excessive eating usually followed by purging. Binge eating usually involves eating high-calorie foods, generally sweets; eating during a time when no one can witness food consumption; ending a binge because of abdominal pain or with vomiting or by sleeping. A person who binge eats usually makes repeated attempts to lose weight, sometimes through excessive exercise, and there are visible signs of frequent weight fluctuations. A bulimic may feel guilty, shameful, and out of control and has low self-esteem. Binge eating can also produce a variety of health problems. Excessive eating can cause problems to the gastrointestinal tract, while the vomiting following the binge eating may cause an electrolyte imbalance and damage the enamel of the teeth. Bulimia should be treated by a qualified professional, and psychotherapy is usually recommended to help with the feelings of low self-esteem associated with the disorder.

Success in Weight Control

Success in weight control depends on being able to choose a program that will lead to life-long, sound nutritional habits. A diet should include foods that are affordable, easy to buy and prepare, and tasty. The caloric value of the foods should provide a weight loss of no more than 1 to 2 pounds per week. It is important to avoid programs that will cause weight loss too quickly with an end result of regaining the lost weight. The main idea is to lose weight and maintain the weight loss. A weight control program should include a form of aerobic exercise a minimum of 3 days a week. Ideally, 4 to 5 days a week of aerobic exercise is recommended for weight loss. However, if the person is beginning a new program from a sedentary state, it is advisable to begin a program and gradually increase the frequency of exercise periods.

Finally, bear in mind that we all have good intentions of eating a nutritionally balanced diet. But even with the best intentions, life's unexpected challenges—busy schedules, trying to lose weight, illness, and stress—can keep you from getting all the proper and necessary nutrition you need. You may want to consult a registered dietitian, sports medicine nutritionist, or physician to evaluate your diet. Most important, try to pay more attention to what you are eating on a daily basis.

Joe Tremaine with his scholarship students in his Los Angeles studio.

CHAPTER 12

*T*HE DANCER'S NEXT STEP

Following an introductory jazz dance course, students may wish to seek additional training in a variety of dance styles as well as opportunities for performance. Most educational settings and private dance studios offer a yearly dance recital or concert for their dance students. With continued training, the dancer may wish to seek a performance opportunity at a dance convention or dance competition. For the serious dance student, there are a variety of career opportunities in the dance world. This chapter addresses these topics for dancers who wish to take the next step.

*A*DDITIONAL TRAINING

With the continued study of jazz dance, the student will recognize the need for additional training in body alignment and dance technique. Jazz dancers may increase their progress by studying ballet in conjunction with jazz dance. Ballet training is extremely beneficial because it focuses on body alignment and the technical analysis of dance steps. Skills learned in ballet class will add clarity to the line and movement of a jazz dancer and will extend the dancer's ability.

Most schools offering jazz dance classes also have ballet classes. It is essential that the student choose a ballet teacher who concentrates on developing technique. The dancer will benefit most from a teacher who stresses proper body placement, with emphasis on individual variations and corrections. A minimum of two ballet lessons per week is suggested for the jazz dancer.

In addition to ballet, the jazz dancer may want to study modern dance. Modern dance expands a dancer's technique and style by incorporating a variety of body positions and movements. It also stresses expression of body language and the use of the elements of dance.

Tap dance is another form that can benefit the jazz dancer. This dance technique emphasizes sharp, fast footwork and encourages awareness of rhythm and syncopation.

JAZZ DANCE PERFORMANCE

Students in a jazz dance class may be given the opportunity to perform in a dance program. For some students, performance will be the highlight of the course, whereas other students may prefer not to be onstage. Students who do not wish to perform can learn a great deal by participating in the production aspects of the dance program.

Behind the Performance Scene

Listed below are jobs for the nonperforming dancer.

- *Publicity*
  Advertisement design and distribution
  Program design and distribution
- *Technical crew*
  Sound
  Lighting
  Costume design and wardrobe assistance
  Props and stage crew
  Makeup
  Ushering
- *Organizing the dance program*
  Title page
  Names of dances
  Name(s) of choreographer(s)
  Cast list

This list may vary, depending on the formality and size of the performance.

Advertisement Design and Distribution

Advertisements should include the title of the concert, performance group, place, date, time, fee, and a telephone number for further information. The design of the advertisement should be clear and easy to read, with a graphic to attract attention. Advertisements should be posted locally and mailed to other dance studios, high schools, and colleges in the vicinity. School and local newspapers should be notified of details regarding the performance. All publicity should be distributed at least three weeks prior to the opening of the performance.

If it is a school performance, flyers can be made using the school's duplicating machine. Large poster advertisements may be made in the school's art department. The art department may be willing to make advertisement design part of a class assignment.

Program Design and Distribution

The design of the program cover may be the same graphic used for advertisements. The program contents should be typed, listing the order of the dances, musical selections, choreographer, and names of dancers appearing in each dance. The production crew should be given credit either at the beginning or at the end of the program. Programs should be made available prior to the concert and may be distributed by the usher.

Sound

Because the music is of utmost importance, a good sound system should be used. In most dance programs, the recording of the sound is done by a single person: the instructor, a member of the school audiovisual department, or a student with the necessary skills. Recording the entire concert on one cassette tape or reel-to-reel recorder is necessary for smooth transitions. Allow short intervals between the selections, record at a consistent volume, and use new records, CDs, or tapes if possible.

Lighting

Lighting for the dance performance may be done by students who are supervised by a person knowledgeable in lighting technique. Someone may be needed in the lighting booth to call cues for lighting, carry out the lighting commands, and run the spotlight. Students who participate in this area of technical operations may also be involved with theater productions or may be nondancers interested in developing this skill.

Costume Design and Wardrobe Assistance

In an informal concert, there may be little money for costuming. If costumes are needed, ingenuity will make something of nothing. Costumes should be kept simple, because changing space and time between dance numbers will be limited.

For costuming group dances, inexpensive material can be used for scarves, sashes, vests, or wrap-around skirts. Old ties can add color and uniformity to the dance group. Brightly colored leotards with matching tights serve as good costumes. Dark leotards with brightly colored accessories can also be used. For solos and duets, the costume list is endless — just visit a secondhand clothing store and a wardrobe can be inexpensively designed. One or more students may be in charge of designing costumes. Students may also assist in the sewing of costumes, or assist dancers with quick costume changes.

Props and Stage Crewing

Some dances require the use of props or sets. Students can be assigned to borrow or make what is needed. The prop manager or an assigned stagehand must place the set or prop in the correct place or be responsible for giving each dancer the prop needed for a specific dance. The stagehand is also responsible for collecting the prop at the end of the dance.

Makeup

The job of the makeup crew may be a fascinating experience for the nondancing student who wants to be involved with dance theater production. The makeup artist is a true artist indeed, working with a wide range of colors to make the face of the dancer an integral part of the dancer's performance. Although for most dances the choreographer will probably request basic stage makeup, sometimes dance themes may lend themselves to elaborate makeup jobs. For even more special effects, body makeup may be used to restate a dance theme.

Ushering

The job of the usher is to direct audience members to their seats and to hand out the dance programs. Ushers should arrive at the theater one hour before the start of the performance and should stand at the head of the aisles or at the entrance to the theater. A dressed-up appearance is appropriate for the usher.

The Performance Space

The dance studio can serve as the performance space for an informal dance concert. A backdrop may be needed to cover the mirror, *barres,* stereo equipment, and so on. A few basic theater lights can be used to highlight the performance area and create a theatrical setting. Chairs with risers provide excellent seating, but chairs alone are adequate.

If it is a school performance and the school has a theater, the concert can be presented in a more formal manner. The technical aspects of the production should be discussed with the person in charge of theater management.

THE DANCE PRODUCTION

Selection of dance pieces for the production and the order of their presentation are integral parts of the dance concert. An informal studio concert may consist of class work and student choreography, with the class warm-up as the show opener. The warm-up should be choreographed with minimal repetitions of movements and should include interesting movement directions, tempo changes, and spatial patterns. The choreographed warm-up may serve as a way to use all dancers. It will require rehearsal so that spacing and musical cues can be set.

A more formal production onstage may be a recital of performance pieces developed specifically for stage performance. Productions may focus on a specific theme, with dance pieces related to that theme by music, choreography, or style. Productions may also present pieces with no common theme.

The order of the program should offer variety. Intersperse solo dances between group dance numbers. Vary the mood by alternating fast and percussive numbers with lyrical dance pieces. Dances with clever costuming or props should be distributed throughout the program. Start and end the program with lively group numbers. The opening dance must immediately capture the attention of the audience. The ending number should be technically sound but highly energetic, for it is what the audience will remember the most.

REHEARSALS AND PERFORMANCE

In addition to numerous rehearsals, at least one nonstop run-through, or dress rehearsal, with costumes, props, and lighting, should occur before the performance. Preferably, this rehearsal should occur the day before the opening date of the concert.

On the day of the performance, it is the dancer's responsibility to arrive at the theater or studio at least one hour before the concert begins, checking in with the teacher or the person in charge. Before the performance, the teacher or a student dance captain may lead a group warm-up. If a group warm-up is not scheduled, it is the dancer's responsibility to warm-up adequately.

A part of the performance warm-up should include your own personal time to prepare mentally for the performance. Focusing your attention to channel your energy in a positive direction will aid your performance. Preperformance anxiety is normal but can hinder performance if it is allowed to overwhelm your emotions. Visualization is an effective means of performance preparation. Concentration must be focused on a successful performance of your dance routine. Imagine yourself performing each movement of the routine perfectly, thus disallowing negative emotions to interfere. The more vivid and detailed your mental routine rehearsal, the better your body is directed in what it needs to do to perform successfully. Visualization makes focusing a positive habit and allows the dancer freedom to be totally involved with the dance, including facial expressions, stylization, and movement dynamics. Just prior to the performance, set aside a time for visualization; imagine your best performance in clear, detailed pictures.

It is normal procedure to begin a performance five minutes after the scheduled time. The technical crew, the backstage crew, and all performers will be alerted prior to the curtain opening. Once the program begins, the continuity of the show should be maintained by minimizing the time between performance pieces. Dancers should be aware of the ongoing stage performance to avoid missing any entrance cues.

At the end of the performance, all dancers come onstage to take their bows. Bows may be simply done, with the entire cast coming forward and bowing in unison. Or, elaborate bows can be choreographed to music, with groups of dancers entering at specific times.

DANCE CONVENTIONS AND COMPETITIONS: AN ALTERNATIVE PERFORMANCE OPPORTUNITY

Dance conventions and competitions are one- to five-day events. Conventions are designed to stimulate the dance instructor and to provide a master-class learning experience for students. Conventions consist of intense training programs and instructional aids such as routine-packed notebooks and videotapes. An integral part of the convention is the final dance competition, where dancers compete in a variety of dance categories for awards. Dancers are judged on technique, execution of movement patterns, rhythm and performance energy, and style; routines are evaluated on their choreographic merit. Currently, there are more than 60 dance conventions a year. Conventions are sponsored nationwide by groups such as Dance Masters of America, Dance America, Hoctor's Dance Caravan, Dance Olympics, World Dance Association, Dupree Dance Conventions, and Joe Tremaine Dance Conventions.

In addition to conventions that include a final competition are organizations that offer strictly competitive events. Competitions are sponsored by groups such as Bravo!, Broadway Bound, Headliners Performing Arts Competition, Rising Star Talent Productions, ShowTime!, Star Power, and a long list of others. Competitions offer a performance opportunity for dancers and a means of evaluating one's own performance skill in relation to a large cross-section of dancers from different parts of the country.

FUTURE IN JAZZ DANCE

There are various career opportunities in the dance world in addition to that of professional performer. Dance talents may also be turned to the professions of dance rehearsal director, choreographer, and teacher. All of these careers require time, energy, ambition, and the patience to endure the technical training necessary to achieve highly developed dance expertise.

Versatility is essential for the dancer. In preparation for any dance career, the dancer should be committed to spending a great deal of time in class study, not only to develop dance skills, but also to develop a variety of dance styles. Singing and acting lessons may also help the dancer in securing work in the theater.

The Professional Dancer

Employment opportunities as a professional dancer include musical theater, film and television (including variety shows, award shows, special programs, and commercials), music videos, cruise line entertainment, cabaret, and nightclub acts. Initially, the dancer must attend as many auditions as possible, including "cattle call" auditions, to gain recognition from choreographers and directors.

On entering the audition, the dancer will be expected to present a résumé and professional photographs. The résumé should include name, address, phone number, hair and eye color (age, height, and weight are optional), and a list of all previous dance work. The professional photographs should include an 8 × 10-inch black-and-white glossy head shot and an 8 × 10-inch black-and-white glossy dance shot, on the bottom of which are listed the dancer's name and union membership. Also included may be four smaller action photographs featuring the dancer's unique dance abilities or photographs of different personality moods, or characteristics, known as a personality composite.

In the warm-up room prior to the audition, it is advisable (and considered good dance etiquette) to find a small corner or side of the room to do warm-up and stretching exercises. Often the warm-up can become a competition between dancers to show off their flexibility, turns, or other dance moves. More experienced dancers may try to use the warm-up to intimidate a dancer new to auditions. Remember the intent of the warm-up period: to prepare yourself physically and mentally for the audition.

Directors and choreographers are often influenced by first impressions. Appearance is a major factor of the first impression. It is important to look neat and clean. Wear dance clothing that flatters your best features and plays down your worst features. It is beneficial for women dancers to show off their legs. Hair should be pulled away from the face but not secured ballet style. Makeup should be heavy day or evening makeup but not stage makeup. To maintain a fresh appearance, bring a towel to wipe perspiration. Finally, absolutely do not chew gum — not even to walk in the door.

Dancers should be prepared with ballet, tap, jazz, character, and tennis shoes. Warm-ups, leg warmers, and sweaters may also be needed for rest periods during the audition.

Generally, an audition call will be for union dancers. If all the dance positions are not selected from the union dancers, then the audition will be open to nonunion dancers. Once a union job is secured, the dancer must join the union associated with the job. Listed below are the various entertainment unions and their areas of concentration.

American Federation of Television and Radio Artists (AFTRA): television and radio, including commercials.

American Guild of Variety Artists (AGVA): nightclub entertainment.

Equity: theater.

Screen Actors Guild (SAG): film, motion pictures, commercials.

Screen Extras Guild (SEG): This is a good union for dancers because extras are less expensive to hire. A dancer may secure a job more easily as an extra than as a dancer merely because the hiring agency does not have to pay as much.

While a dancer is concentrating on obtaining professional dance work, there are other nonprofessional opportunities available. A growing number of dance companies perform and tour. There are also special presentations of choreographers' new works. Although many of these jobs are done for free or with little pay, they offer the beginning dance performer an opportunity to gain exposure and performance practice.

Finally, the aspiring dancer must have a standby job to cover living expenses while developing a professional career. The job should have flexible hours so that the dancer can attend auditions.

Any dancer interested in pursuing a dance career would benefit by reading the following books: *The Dancer's Survival Manual* by Marian Horosko and Judith Kupersmith; *The Dancer's Audition Book* by Martin

A. David; and *Dance Auditions: Preparations, Presentations, Career Planning* by Eric B. Nielsen.

The Dance Rehearsal Director

Many choreographers teach the dances at the first few rehearsals and then return at a later date to view the progress of the dancers and to make auditions and corrections to the dances. The most proficient dancer or a dancer that has previously worked with the choreographer conducts most of the rehearsals. That dancer is designated as the dance captain or dance rehearsal director.

The Choreographer

In most cases, a choreographer was once a professional dancer who left the performance spotlight, first to teach, then to become an assistant choreographer, and finally to become a choreographer. A choreographer usually begins a career by working for community theaters, dance companies, colleges, junior colleges, or high schools. At first, some work may be done for limited pay, for expenses, or for free. A choreographer's success depends on the response of people in the production end of the entertainment world. Choreographers should become acquainted with directors, producers, theater owners and leaders of theater organizations, and department chairpersons. These people should be invited to any concerts or theatrical work done by the choreographer.

Work in choreography may also be found with a touring dance convention for teachers, students, and professional groups. Choreographers are paid a substantial fee for a two- or three-day presentation on choreography. Examples of such dance clinic groups are listed under dance conventions.

Other choreography jobs may be found at summer dance camps. Here the talents of choreographer, teacher, and dance rehearsal director must be combined in choreographing and directing dance routines for local groups. In addition, they are expected to give lectures and demonstrations in makeup, auditioning, dance technique, and choreography. The culmination of the dance camp clinic is a competitive performance by the student dance groups, which are judged on choreography, dance technique and execution, appearance, projection, and esprit de corps.

The Dance Teacher

Dance teaching is perhaps the most secure profession in the dancer's world. A jazz dance teacher may find employment on a full-time or part-time basis in private or professional dance studios, in educational settings, and in recreation departments. Students may range from children to adults, and abilities from novice to advanced.

Proficiency in dance technique is required for all teaching positions. At the public high school level, a dance teacher must have a secondary-level teaching credential. At the junior college and college level, a dance teacher must have a master's degree. In some instances, a master's degree may be waived if a dancer has had extensive professional dance experience. Colleges and universities may encourage instructors to continue their education toward a doctorate (Ph.D.) and may expect them to contribute to dance research and publications.

Another teaching area the jazz dance instructor may wish to investigate is the increasingly popular fitness form of jazz dance. Because of the dancer's extensive training in movement and technique, teaching aerobic dance classes can be a smooth transition. The popularity of aerobic dance provides a wide range of employment opportunities.

In any teaching situation, it is the personality, knowledge, and abilities of the teacher that sustain a class. An ability to analyze and clarify movement and technique is essential for good teaching. A clear understanding of the needs of a student must also be developed.

Although not all dancers may choose a professional career, dance in itself is a medium that gives physical, mental, and emotional fulfillment at whatever level it is pursued.

APPENDIX

JAZZ DANCE STYLES

Although technique is the foundation of dance, performance is characterized by style. Jazz dance, through stylization, has become as individualized and as important a means of personal expression as modern dance. For example, a basic jazz walk can take on many attitudes depending on the style that the performer interprets. Each teacher will also have his or her own individual style. The aspect of dance that is called "style" is a combination of influences that all contribute to the uniqueness and variety of jazz.

Because jazz dance has so many influences from theater, social dance, and classical dance, many styles have become recognizable and have been given a descriptive name. This section discusses the major styles of contemporary jazz dance. New influences and new styles will be created in the future.

Lyrical Jazz

Lyrical jazz is strongly influenced by ballet. Its movements use the entire body, extending the body lines. Movements possess a flowing quality, although a strong pulse may be used to emphasize dynamics. Sharp angular movements are generally avoided. The Luigi technique relates to lyrical jazz. Luigi combinations employ ballet technique but are performed with asymmetrical body lines, increased and varied movements of the spine, and syncopated rhythms and movements.

Musical Comedy or Theater Jazz

Musical comedy, or theater jazz, is the style of jazz usually performed on the Broadway stage and in early dance musicals. Theater jazz is characterized by movements that assist the story line of the play or musical. Often, the dance is an interaction of the characters of the play in relation to the story's plot.

Musical comedy jazz dance often incorporates props: hats, canes, chairs, and other objects relating to the story line of the play.

New York and London are the hubs of musical comedy jazz, and many well-known masters of this style make their homes there.

Funk Jazz

Funk jazz is often referred to as L.A. jazz dance, although dance studios across the United States teach it. Compared with lyrical jazz dance, funk jazz is angular and disjointed. It employs hip isolations, shoulder shrugs, and head rolls. Dance movements tend to be pedestrian, emphasizing walking, hand clapping, finger snapping, and general body isolations. Many of its dance steps come from social dance: the jitterbug, the two-step, the frug.

Modern Jazz

Modern jazz dance is heavily influenced by modern dance. It uses body contractions, flexed feet, and off-center body shapes, which are reflective of modern dance techniques. This style of jazz dance may be more pre-dominantly performed in concert or studio recitals as opposed to the styles of jazz dance used for Broadway shows, music videos, or television and commercial specials. This style may be more expressive and follows the exercise techniques of modern dance disciplines.

Hip Hop/Street Funk

Hip hop/street funk, a form of street dance, is the newest trend in jazz dance. The movements are bouncy, fast, and funky. Hip hop/street funk is extremely foot oriented but uses isolation movements, popping, and breakdancing. Hip hop/street funk moves to a syncopated beat—a rhythmic shuffle beat, evident in hip hop music. Hip hop/street funk is highly energetic and allows the dancer to improvise and perform with freedom of movement.

Jazz dance style is constantly changing. New innovations in style, technique, and choreography continue to emerge on the jazz dance scene. Students should seek training in a variety of styles to experience a variety of challenges and to maximize self-expression.

BIBLIOGRAPHY

CHAPTER 1: JAZZ DANCE: A HISTORY

Billington, Michael. *Performing Arts*. New York: Facts on File, 1980.

Bauer, B. "Jazz Energy—Joe Tremaine." *Dance Teacher Now* (September-October 1984): 14–21.

Colby, Peter W. "Tremaine Dance Conventions." *Dancer* (September 1994): 27.

De Mille, Agnes. *America Dances*. New York: Macmillan, 1980.

Ellfeldt, Lois. *Dance: From Magic to Art*. Dubuque, Iowa: Brown, 1976.

Emery, Lynne Fauley. *Black Dance in the United States from 1619 to 1970*. Palo Alto, Calif.: Mayfield, 1972.

Giordano, Gus. *Anthology of American Jazz Dance*. Evanston, Ill.: Orion, 1978.

Greenhill, Janet. "Joe Tremaine and L.A. Jazz." *Dance Teacher Now* (March 1994): 47–51.

Grubb, Kevin. "Dance Films '85." *Dance Magazine* (December 1984): 84–87.

Grubb, Kevin. "Basil Blasts Off." *Dance Magazine* (March 1988): 62–68.

Gruen, John. "Britain's Broadway Blitz." *Dance Magazine* (July 1988): 42–45.

Horosko, Marian. "The Jazz Dance Kings." *Dance Magazine* (April 1991): 66–67.

Jackson, Michael. *Smooth Criminal*. Ultimate Productions, 1988.

Jackson, Michael. *Michael Jackson, The Legend Continues*. Motown on Showtime, MSS/Optimum Productions, 1988.

Jackson, Michael. *History: Michael Jackson's Greatest Video Hits*. Epic Music Video, 1995.

Kelly, Kelvin. "Tony, Emmy, Oscar, and Bob," in Broadway show program of *Dancin'*, 1978.

Luigi, and Wydro, Kenneth. *The Luigi Jazz Dance Technique*. Garden City, N.Y.: Doubleday, 1981.

Missett, Judi Sheppard. *Jazzercise*. New York: Bantam Books, 1978.

Thomas, Tony. *That's Dancing*. New York: Abrams, 1984.

Time-Life Books, *LIFE Goes to the Movies*. New York: Time-Life Books, 1975.

Pierpont, Margaret. "Joe Tremaine: A Drive for Jazz." *Dance Magazine* (December 1983): 100–101.

Rosenwald, Peter J. "Breakaway '80's Style." *Dance Magazine* (April 1984): 70–84.

Wolgemuth, Ruth. "Joe Tremaine—L.A. Dance Award's Educators Award." *Kickline* (January-February 1995).

CHAPTER 3: A DANCER'S ALIGNMENT

Drury, Blanche. *Posture and Figure Control Through Physical Education*. Palo Alto, Calif.: National Press Publishing, 1970.

Fitt, Sally Sevey. *Dance Kinesiology*. New York: Schirmer Books, 1988.

Rathbone, Josephine, and Hunt, Valerie. *Corrective Physical Education*. Philadelphia: Saunders, 1985.

Sweigard, Lulu E. *Human Movement Potential*. New York: Dodd, Mead, 1974.

Todd, Mabel. *The Thinking Body*. New York: Dance Horizons, 1937.

Wells, Katherine F. *Kinesiology*. Philadelphia: Saunders, 1971.

CHAPTER 4: BALLET FOR THE JAZZ DANCER

Grant, Gail. *Technical Manual and Dictionary of Classical Ballet*. New York: Dover, 1967.

Hammond, Sandra Noll. *Ballet Basics*. Palo Alto, Calif.: Mayfield, 1974.

Hammond, Sandra Noll. *Ballet: Beyond the Basics*. Palo Alto, Calif.: Mayfield, 1982.

Kirstein, Lincoln, Stuart, Muriel, and Dyer, Carlus. *The Classic Ballet: Basic Technique and Terminology*. New York: Knopf, 1977.

Shook, Karel. *Elements of Classical Ballet Technique*. New York: Dance Horizons, 1977.

Vaganova, Agrippina. *Basic Principles of Classical Ballet*. New York: Dover, 1969.

CHAPTER 5: BASIC JAZZ POSITIONS

Giordano, Gus. *Anthology of American Jazz Dance*. Evanston, Ill.: Orion, 1978.

Traguth, Fred. *Modern Jazz Dance*. New York: Dance Motion Press, 1978.

CHAPTER 6: THE JAZZ DANCE WARM-UP

Alter, Michael J. *Science of Stretching*. Champaign, Ill.: Human Kinetics Books, 1988.

Giordano, Gus. *Anthology of American Jazz Dance*. Evanston, Ill.: Orion, 1978.

Hutchinson, Ann. *Labanotation*. New York: Dance Notation Bureau, 1970.

Kinkead, Mary Ann. *Elementary Labanotation*. Palo Alto, Calif.: Mayfield, 1982.

Martin, B. J. "Effect of Warm-Up on Metabolic Responses to Strenuous Exercise." *Medicine in Science and Sports* (no. 2, 1975): 146–149.

Sienna, Phillip. *One Rep Max*. Carmel, Ind.: Benchmark Press, 1989.

CHAPTER 7: BASIC JAZZ DANCE

Frich, Elisabeth. *The Matt Mattox Book of Jazz Dance*. New York: Sterling. 1983.

Sabatine, Jean. *Technique and Styles of Jazz Dancing*. Waldwick, N.J.: Hocter Dance Records, 1969.

CHAPTER 9: PUTTING IT ALL TOGETHER

Ammer, Christine. *Harper's Dictionary of Music*. New York: Harper & Row, 1972.

Dimondstein, Geraldine. *Children Dance in the Classroom*. New York: Macmillan, 1971.

Hayes, Elizabeth. *Dance Composition and Production*. New York: Ronald Press, 1955.

Lockhart, Aileene. *Modern Dance*. Dubuque, Iowa: Brown, 1966.

Murray, Ruth. *Dance in Elementary Education*. New York: Harper & Row, 1953.

Sherbon, Elizabeth. *On the Count of One: Modern Dance Methods,* 3rd edition. Palo Alto, Calif.: Mayfield, 1982.

CHAPTER 10: FITNESS FOR THE JAZZ DANCER

Corbin, Charles B., and Lindsey, Ruth. *Concepts of Fitness*. Dubuque, Iowa: Brown, 1985.

Fox, Edward L., Bowers, Richard W., and Foss, Merle L. *The Physiological Basis of Physical Education and Athletics,* 4th edition. Philadelphia: Saunders, 1988.

Jensen, Clayne R., and Fisher, Garth A. *Scientific Basis of Athletic Conditioning,* 2nd edition. Philadelphia: Lea and Febiger, 1979.

Lamb, David R. *Physiology of Exercise: Response and Adaptations,* 2nd edition. New York: Macmillan, 1984.

McArdle, William D., Frank, I., and Katch, Victor L. *Exercise Physiology: Energy, Nutrition, and Human Performance*. Philadelphia: Lea and Febiger, 1981.

Williams, Melvin. *Lifetime Physical Fitness*. Dubuque, Iowa: Brown, 1985.

CHAPTER 11: THE DANCER'S INSTRUMENT: TAKING CARE OF IT

Allsen, Phillip E., Harrison, Joyce M., and Vance, Barbara. *Fitness for Life: An Individualized Approach*. Dubuque, Iowa: Brown, 1975.

Angeline, Karen. "Vitamins A to Zinc." *Women's Sports and Fitness* (March 1992): 20, 22.

Bailey, Covert. *Fit or Fat?* Boston: Houghton Mifflin, 1977.

Benjamin, Ben E. *Sports Without Pain*. New York: Summit Books, 1979.

Bogert, L. Jean, Briggs, George M., and Calloway, Dorris Howes. *Nutrition and Physical Fitness*. Philadelphia: Saunders, 1966.

Bucher, Charles A., and Prentice, William E. *Fitness for College and Life*. St. Louis: Times/Mirror, Mosby, 1985.

Calbom, Cherie. "Drink Your Vegetables." *Women's Sports and Fitness* (September 1992): 26, 28.

Cantu, Robert C. *Sports Medicine in Primary Care*. Lexington, Mass.: Heath, 1982.

Chronicle Wire Services. "One or Two Drinks May Break Up Blood Clots." *Chronicle* (September 28, 1994).

Francis, Lorna L. *Injury Prevention Manual for Dance Exercise.* San Diego: National Injury Prevention Foundation, 1983.

International BioAnalogics Systems, Inc. "Body Composition Techniques," 1992.

King, Janet C., Cohenour, Sally H., Corruccini, Carol G., and Schneernan, Paul. "Evaluation and Modification of the Basic Four Food Guide." *Journal of Nutrition Education* (vol. 10, no. 1, 1978): 27–29.

Klafs, Carl E., and Arnheim, Daniel D. *Modern Principles of Athletic Training.* St. Louis: Mosby, 1969.

McArdle, William D., Katch, Frank I., and Katch, Victor I. *Exercise Physiology: Energy, Nutrition, and Human Performance.* Philadelphia: Lee & Febiger, 1981.

Miller, David K., and Allen, T. Earl. *Fitness: A Lifetime Commitment.* Minneapolis, Minn.: Burgess, 1979.

Mott, Jane A. *Conditioning and Basic Movement Concepts.* Dubuque, Iowa: Brown, 1968.

Somer, Elizabeth. *Nutrition for Women: The Complete Guide.* Henry Holt and Co., 1993.

Thomas, Dana. "Exercise—Nature's Prozac." *Self* (July 1994): 71–73, 132.

Whitney, Eleanore Noss, and Hamilton, Eva May. *Nutrition: Concepts and Controversies.* St. Paul, Minn.: West, 1982.

Williams, Melvin. *Lifetime Physical Fitness.* Dubuque, Iowa: Brown, 1985.

NDEX